INDUSTRIALIZING AMERICA

INDUSTRIALIZING AMERICA

Understanding Contemporary Society through Classical Sociological Analysis

Frank W. Elwell

Westport, Connecticut
London

Library of Congress Cataloging-in-Publication Data

Elwell, Frank W.
Industrializing America : understanding contemporary society through classical sociological analysis / Frank W. Elwell.
p. cm.
Includes bibliographical references and index.
ISBN 0–275–96563–5 (alk. paper). — ISBN 0–275–96564–3 (pbk. : alk. paper)
1. Sociology 2. Social sciences—Philosophy. 3. United States—Social conditions—1980– I. Title.
HM24.E46 1999
301—dc21 99–12682

British Library Cataloguing in Publication Data is available.

Library of Congress Catalog Card Number: 99–12682
ISBN: 0–275–96563–5
0–275–96564–3 (pbk.)

First published in 1999

Praeger Publishers, 88 Post Road West, Westport, CT 06881
An imprint of Greenwood Publishing Group, Inc.
www.praeger.com

Printed in the United States of America

The paper used in this book complies with the Permanent Paper Standard issued by the National Information Standards Organization (Z39.48–1984).

10 9 8 7 6 5 4 3 2 1

For Patricia

Within the realm of social conduct one finds factual regularities, that is, courses of action which, with a typically identical meaning, are repeated by the actors or simultaneously occur among numerous actors. It is with such types of conduct that sociology is concerned, in contrast to history, which is interested in the causal connections of important, i.e., fateful, single events.

— Max Weber (1921)

Turning and turning in the widening gyre
The falcon cannot hear the falconer
Things fall apart: the center cannot hold;
Here anarchy is loosed upon the world.
The blood-dimmed tide is loosed, and everywhere
The ceremony of innocence is drowned;
The best lack all conviction, while the worst
Are full of passionate intensity.

— W. B. Yeats (1924)*

Contents

Preface

The intent of this book is to present a comprehensive (and comprehensible) vision of the sociocultural system. To do this I open with a theoretical chapter and then use the theory to analyze industrial systems — particularly the advanced system in the United States. I open with social theory with some trepidation. It has been my experience that most American students loathe and fear social theory (at one time I could count myself in this group), and I fear many will not get past the first chapter. To counter this, I have attempted to present the theory as clearly and forthrightly as possible, but it still might throw some who prefer more concrete analysis. For those readers who are thrown by the theoretical discussion, I advise you to begin with Chapter 2 and return to Chapter 1 after you finish the book. The illustrations of the theory encountered in chapters 2–8 will make the theory in Chapter 1 more easily comprehensible. I believe strongly in the usefulness of social theory. An explicit framework of the sociocultural whole is invaluable in understanding any one part of society. Getting that message across — whatever route the reader takes — is the overriding goal of this work.

Before going any further into the book I also acknowledge my stand on politically correct language — particularly as it relates to gender-neutral and gender-inclusive terms. When I use such terms as "man" and "mankind" (instead of "humankind"), I intend to include both genders unless I specifically state otherwise. As evidence of this good faith effort

I often go on to use the pronoun she to refer to man and mankind. For example, I may write: "Although man may have some simple reflex actions to stimuli from her environment, she is relatively free from biological instincts and predispositions." This startles many of my students. The reason I do this is twofold: The language is beautiful and should not be changed by committee — there is a certain elegance in mankind that is lacking in humankind. More important, by using such terms as "mankind" and referring to these terms and other social groupings with sometimes feminine and sometimes masculine pronouns and possessives, I am connecting to the traditions of my culture and reinterpreting them at the same time. This, it seems to me, is the shortest route to what we should all be interested in achieving — a language that is inclusive and does not rank more than half of the human population as second class. If living languages change in the same manner as other types of social change, redefining the meaning of terms occurs far more often than coining new ones.

Acknowledgments

I have discussed the ideas in this book over the years with many colleagues and students, and even a few casual acquaintances and strangers. Many of these people stretched my mind, and I thank them. I also appreciate all my family and friends for their social and emotional support. Without trying to shift onto them any of the blame, I express my debt to a few friends by name, friends who went beyond the call in challenging me to develop and refine the ideas expressed in this book. They include Michael Miller, Lillian Daughaday, and Gayne Nerney (all of Murray State University); David Slausen; and David Biernoff (of the University of Southern Queensland). I also owe a debt to my family as well as these same friends and others (including Duke Wilder and Chris Royere) who gave me the emotional and social support I needed. Finally, I publicly thank Eva King, who tried to protect the English language from my occasional assaults on its integrity. Although the faults are mine, these people gave aid and comfort.

Introduction

This book is addressed to students of society, both those who are formally enrolled in undergraduate and graduate courses and those who are on a more independent journey. I have always been fascinated with human society, with not only the incredible variety but also the underlying conformity of human behavior. My discipline, sociology, has served me well in pursuing this passion. The sociological literature has provided me with concepts, insights, empirical findings, and theories that have helped me make sense of the social world. This, I believe, is the major task and promise of sociology — to construct a symbolic framework that will allow us to understand social life better. Through this understanding we can more realistically confront the problems of our social life together.

I fear that many sociologists and students are losing sight of this task. Like society itself, sociology is experiencing an increasing division of labor as evidenced by the increase in the number of specialties within the discipline. The American Sociological Association currently recognizes more than 30 of these specialties, and a look at the curricula vitae of young sociologists provides evidence that these specialties will continue to multiply in the future. Coupled with this specialization is also an increasing fragmentation within the discipline. Many of us rarely read outside our specialties. Sociological specialists seldom relate their expertise in one institutional order to the total sociocultural system. The construction and study of sociological theory itself has become a specialty, often focusing on points of historical interest and providing little guidance to researchers investigating such areas as aging, criminology, education, or the family.

Instead of relating our research within the larger social context, we have become so specialized and focused on our substantive area that we are in danger of losing our vision of the system as a whole. Many of our texts in introductory sociology and social problems are a compendium of facts and seemingly conflicting middle-range theories of 12 to 22 specialties (the number and specific specialty tend to vary with fashion). One chapter discusses aging, the next stratification, and the next gender studies. There is little connection of the findings in one specialty with those in another. Worse, there is little attempt to relate the findings to any comprehensive sociological world view. There is also a marked trend in our undergraduate texts to focus on social psychology — microperspectives that American students can readily identify with — rather than attempt the more difficult task of presenting and defending a comprehensive macro-perspective that will help make sense of social stability and social change. Some books do go through the motions, often by presenting the two macrotheories of functionalism and conflict theory. Most of these discussions, however, make it plain that both perspectives are incomplete visions of the social whole, grafted onto textbook discussions of empirical findings and middle-range theories almost as an afterthought.

Instead of presenting a comprehensive macroscopic theory of social stability and change we encourage our students to be eclectic — that is, adopt any theory (often of the middle-range variety) that seems to explain the phenomenon under study. When we change the phenomenon under study, we change the theory. Marvin Harris (1979, 287–288) labels such eclecticism a scientific disaster, virtually guaranteeing middle-range theories without end and incoherence within the discipline as a whole. Indeed, the goal of understanding society appears increasingly unattainable as we look at the sheer volume of economic, political, social, physical, and psychological factors advanced by numerous theories — some contradictory — to explain sociocultural phenomena. Although eclecticism has served sociology well in terms of the proliferation of research tasks, middle-range theories, and specialization, it has not significantly advanced students' (or sociologists') understanding of sociocultural systems as a whole. This, I think, is a disservice to our students and to our discipline.

I believe that our present confusion is not simply the result of the complexity of our subject matter, but is in large measure the unsystematic way we study and present it. To provide coherence we must go back to our roots; back to the classical tradition. This tradition should not be examined as just another specialty or taught only in one course as history unrelated to the modern discipline. Rather, this tradition, and its modern-day expressions, should be examined for their truths, relevance, and insight into the present social world. Much is there. Although there is some that is of little value (aside from historical interest) much of the classical tradition in sociology is profound in its relevance.

What is also remarkable about this tradition is that there is much commonality in the theories and insights of our founders. While they often focused on different aspects of the social system and had the unfortunate tendency to coin their own concepts and develop their theories in isolation from one another, there is a more consistent sociological perspective than many realize. Several modern-day sociologists and anthropologists have engaged in attempting to synthesize this tradition into a more coherent, comprehensive vision of social stability and change. Among them I would list Marvin Harris and Gerhard and Jean Lenski. In our recent past I would also include the work of C. Wright Mills, a postwar American sociologist who attempted to synthesize such classical theoriests as Marx and Weber. All of these social scientists have used the classical tradition — borrowed from such titans as Karl Marx, Max Weber, T. Robert Malthus, Emile Durkheim, and Herbert Spencer — to construct a comprehensive vision of the social world. This book represents my attempt to build upon these efforts and continue this tradition — and then to apply this sociological perspective to making sense of the modern world. This, I believe, is the major task of the discipline — it should be our promise to our students as well.

Dye

THE SYSTEM

This book begins with a single premise: that society is a system. This means that the various components of society fit together; that whenever a change occurs in one part of the social system it inevitably affects other parts of the system. As ecologists are fond of saying, "we can't do one thing." For students of sociology, this means that we cannot achieve an understanding of social phenomena without reference to the whole sociocultural system and its history; to have relevance, we cannot continue to study society by breaking it down into specialties and leaving it to experts who talk only to themselves. This book is not addressed to those specialists. Rather, it is written for the generalists — for those students of society who want to explore how the social studies can add to our understanding of the social world ("social studies" in Mills's sense of the term — a more inclusive term of what social scientists actually do). The goals of this book are to summarize a comprehensive systems-theory of society and then to use the theory to understand advanced industrial societies. By understand, I mean to make sense of industrial society by relating the seeming chaos to a logically consistent framework.

My chief concerns can be summarized by the questions, How is social order maintained in societies through time? and How and why do societies change? In addressing these questions it is not my intent to discount the rôle of biology, psychology, or history in human social behavior. Although the focus of this book is on sociocultural systems, I recognize that human social behavior is the result of a complex web of social, cultural, historical, biological, and psychological forces that act both independently and with one another to affect (or effect) human behavior. Nor is this book a plaintive whine about how we are all victimized by "the system" — it is not meant to excuse criminal, deviant, or conforming behavior. By writing about social causation I am not attacking the concept of free will and asserting that we should not hold individuals accountable for their actions. Whether or not "free will" exists (perhaps it is only a label that we give to biological, social, and psychological forces and their interactions within individuals), one of the social forces that holds a society together is individual accountability for actions. By describing a sociocultural system that pushes and channels people into certain behaviors the reader should not construe that sociologists are trying to excuse that behavior; rather, they are only trying to explain it (if you thought otherwise, you might have us confused with psychologists). Such explanations can then be used to understand the social system better and, it is hoped, to effect structural reform that is consistent with social justice.

It should also be pointed out that no social theory could possibly account for all of the similarity and diversity of social life. Social life is complex, and any theory that attempted such a feat would be of little use in our attempts to understand social reality (because its complexity would approach social reality itself). What is possible, I believe, is the development of a theory that allows students and investigators to visualize the whole and how the various parts fit into that whole — a theoretical framework that attempts to organize the most important components of sociocultural systems and sketches out their reciprocal relationships with one another.

Such a theory can serve as a guide in organizing our perceptions, which allow us to integrate facts, relationships, and insights into a comprehensive and consistent framework. This framework, it should be understood, is to be modified as new observations and insights warrant. Its primary purpose is to provide a world view that summarizes and makes sense of the social world. Such a social world view will then be useful in guiding the research programs of men and women in social studies and provide an understanding of social life for our students. Social theory, much like evolutionary theory in biology, serves as the organizing framework; one that does not provide all of the answers but that informs practitioners and students what to look for and the mechanisms to integrate new information. Should there be significant reliable information that runs counter to theoretical expectations, only then should the theory be modified, or, if called for, abandoned for a new one.

Theory in science (both natural and social), like other forms of technology, seeks to simplify. Sociological theory attempts to simplify social reality by considering only a limited number of variables, the primary factors, in explaining the phenomenon under study. The usefulness of a social theory can be measured by its simplicity and clarity of expression and by the range of social life that can be included in its scope. Good social theory is both simple and powerful. The theoretical perspective presented in these pages is my synthesis of the theories and social insights of numerous sociologists and anthropologists. This framework, I believe, provides a useful starting point in understanding the organization, maintenance, and change of sociocultural systems.

In examining the social structure and culture of modern industrial societies I have relied heavily on many of the concepts and social theories of the founders of my discipline — particularly those of Max Weber. Sociology was founded in response to the social turmoil produced by the initial waves of the industrial revolution. Institutions of property, community, family, and government were shaken to their very core; longstanding cultural traditions and values were abrogated or modified beyond recognition. As this book will make clear, the industrial revolution is ongoing — many of the core concepts and posited relationships of the classical tradition are still central in understanding contemporary sociocultural systems. Beginning with a theoretical base from Marvin Harris (who combines the sociologies of Marx and Malthus) I have integrated many of these key concepts and theories, those that seem particularly useful in understanding the organization and change in modern industrial societies.

The theory begins with the assertion that change in social structures, cultural values, and ideologies are interrelated and rooted in massive growth in population and industrial processes (population and production variables are included in the term "infrastructure"). The recent growth of social infrastructures throughout the world has been massive. World population growth is still averaging about 1.8 percent per year; the population is about 5.6 billion people and doubling in size about every 40 years (Brown, Kane, & Roodman, 1995, 99). World economic growth, although recently slowing, is about 2 to 3 percent per year (a doubling time of about 25 to 35 years) (p. 73). Through rapid growth of both population and production we are causing massive changes in social structures (human groups and organizations) and cultural superstructures (values, beliefs, norms, and ideologies). By introducing this rapid growth into the foundation of sociocultural systems — a process that began some 200 years ago, but which has reached exponential rates today — we are transforming the character of that system. We cannot do one thing.

SOCIAL CHANGE AND SOCIAL PROBLEMS

For those of us who are concerned with social problems, a system view has practical importance. A system view leads to the realization that social problems are usually not the result of some malfunctioning part, but are a consequence of the sociocultural system itself. In order to understand social problems, we must first understand the sociocultural system that creates these problems. If these connections are not made clear, solutions become impossible. You cannot reform the educational system in isolation from the family or the economy; you cannot solve the family "crisis" in modern society without reforming the economy, government policies, or our relationship with work. By understanding the web of interaction between various parts of the sociocultural system, we can adequately address our social problems. This knowledge is essential if we hope to achieve a more just and humane society.

There is a reciprocal relationship between social change and social problems. Social change often causes social problems; these problems, in turn, often cause further social change. It has often been asserted that change is accelerating in modern society; it also has been asserted that our social problems appear to be multiplying. There is a connection in the two trends. More than this, many perceive a qualitative difference in the social problems we face today. Because of the sheer size of our population and the power of our technology, we now pose a direct threat to the environment that sustains us. Environmental degradation brought about by increasing population and growing industrialism has reached crisis proportions in many regions of the world (indeed, the crisis has become worldwide with greenhouse gases and ozone depletion). Other problems are associated with access to valuable resources. There is gross inequality within societies, which appears to be growing. Whether its cause is racism, sexism, religious intolerance, or classism, all societies provide differential access to employment — poverty falls on some groups far more heavily than on others. There is gross inequality between societies as well. Again, this inequality seems to be greater today than at any previous time in human history. Other problems are associated with the decline of family and community and the rise of formal organizations. Many people have remarked about a dehumanizing trend in modern society, a trend that devalues human initiative, freedom, autonomy, and relationships. Still other problems appear to plague the individual. These problems include criminal and sexual deviance; alcohol and drug abuse; teenage pregnancy; suicide; and high levels of alienation, apathy, and consumerism — all of which appear to be approaching epidemic levels in many industrial nations.

The claim of this book is that it is the massive growth of infrastructures that cause both structural and cultural change. Some social problems are the direct, often unintended consequence of technological and demographic change; still others are a consequence of changes in social structures and cultural value systems in interaction with this technological and demographic growth. We pay a sociocultural cost for infrastructural growth. We cannot do one thing.

C. Wright Mills, a Weberian scholar and social critic, wrote of the relevance of the sociological tradition to understanding contemporary society, to understanding the central problems of our time:

> No problem can be adequately formulated unless the values involved and the apparent threat to them are stated. These values and their imperilment constitute the terms of the problem itself. The values that have been the thread of classic social analysis, I believe, are freedom and reason; the forces that imperil them today seem at times to be co-extensive with the major trends of contemporary society, if not to constitute the characterizing features of the contemporary period. The leading problems of the social studies today have this in common: They concern conditions and tendencies that seem to imperil these two values and the consequences of that imperilment for the nature of man and the making of history. (Mills 1959, 129–130)

We learn from Mills, as we did from Weber before him, that the forces that today imperil individual freedom and reason lie in the growth of bureaucracy, a rational social organization, which is designed to coordinate and control the actions of men and women. "It is not too much to say that in the extreme development the chance to reason of most men is destroyed, as rationality increases and its locus, its control, is moved from the individual to the big-scale organization. There is then rationality without reason. Such rationality is not commensurate with freedom but the destroyer of it" (Mills 1959, 170). The rise of formal rationality and its effects on human reason and freedom; on the social bonds of religious and ethical values, traditions, and emotional commitment to one another, is the continuing theme of this book.

1

Sociocultural Materialism: A Sociological Revision

It is my belief that the social studies would benefit from an explicit theory that integrates many of the insights and theories of all the disciplines in a comprehensive yet understandable fashion. Such a theory would be useful in teaching, in research, and in our attempts to make our discipline accessible to a broader audience. I believe that sociocultural materialism, a theory that synthesizes the insights of many social theorists and observers, could serve such a function. The theory is sufficiently broad and flexible to encompass the work and views of a significant proportion of social scientists. At the same time, I believe the theory of sociocultural materialism can provide the theoretical discipline that is needed to systematize our observations of social life.

In America, social theory is about as popular as a root canal. In fact, I suspect that many students would prefer root canal work rather than endure another discussion of functionalism or conflict theory. Perhaps this is because social theories have become divorced from social reality. Sociocultural materialism, however, is easily comprehensible and readily lends itself to an understanding of our world. As a social theory, it offers a usable, coherent, and comprehensive framework that summarizes the complex web of interrelationships that make up social systems. As a contemporary theory, it is based on social insights of the past as well as recent empirical findings. It is an attempt to account for the origin, maintenance, and change of societies.

Social reality is just too complex to grasp without a working outline that points to the interrelationships of social structures and culture. A theory is needed that informs observers how society is organized, how it changes over time, and how this structure and change affect human behaviors. Without an adequate framework, popular understanding becomes confused; reform becomes chaotic; democracy becomes a sham. Social theory, although not popular, could be one of the most relevant subjects of our time.

BIOLOGICAL AND PSYCHOLOGICAL NEEDS

Sociocultural materialism begins with the assertion that human beings are motivated to satisfy biological and psychological needs. Whereas the needs are universal, the ways in which people meet their needs, as well as the extent to which their needs are met, are highly variable. Mankind is relatively free from biological instincts, drives, and predispositions. Rather than relying on instinctive behavior, we learn the repertoire of our social behavior. Sociocultural systems have a dramatic effect on how people satisfy their biopsychological needs or constants.

According to Marvin Harris (1979) there are four biopsychological constants that concern us:

> 1) People need to eat and will generally opt for diets that offer more rather than fewer calories and proteins and other nutrients.
>
> 2) People cannot be totally inactive, but when confronted with a given task, they prefer to carry it out by expending less rather than more [human] energy.
>
> 3) People are highly sexed and generally find reinforcing pleasure from sexual intercourse — more often from heterosexual intercourse. [I disagree with Harris on this last part, I believe that the form of expression of our sexuality is learned.]
>
> 4) People need love and affection in order to feel secure and happy, and other things being equal, they will act to increase the love and affection which others give them. (Harris 1979, 63)

Harris justifies his list with two observations: first, that humans share these biological and psychological needs with other primates; thus, the list's universality is virtually assured. Second, the list should not be judged on its inclusiveness but on the adequacies of theories it helps to generate. There are, of course, other biological and psychological needs — sleep and elimination of waste, for example — but rather than enumerate them all, the focus is on a parsimonious list of assumptions needed to account for the similarities and differences of human behavior. The goal of any social theory is brevity. The fewer the assumptions and statements needed to account for social reality, the more powerful the theory is.

It is through socialization and interaction that we learn culturally approved ways of satisfying our biological and psychological needs. In American society many people have been so successful in satisfying their need for food and reduced energy expenditure that some are opting for restricted diets and exercise. That this goes counter to our biological and psychological predisposition is evidenced in that both take an extreme amount of discipline (discipline that many of us are unable to master). That people are highly sexed cannot be denied. When compared with other primates, we appear to have a very strong sex drive (though I understand that compared with pygmy chimpanzees we are almost asexual in nature). That the human sex drive is channeled by culture so that we learn varying ways of sexual satisfaction also is well established in literature. Of the four needs, only one needs further explanation — the need for affection.

Walter Goldschmidt, an ecological anthropologist, believes that the human need for affection is so important that he makes it the centerpiece of his anthropology. Citing the work of Harry Harlow (1959) on rhesus monkeys and Rene Spitz (1965) on affection-starved human infants, Goldschmidt concludes that satisfying the need for affection is critical for both psychological and physical health. It is this affection need by infants, he believes, that is the central mechanism in the socialization process in which an infant internalizes the culture of a group. In response to affection from others, Goldschmidt posits, an infant makes social rules, roles, values, and beliefs her own.

In adult life the affection need is satisfied through acquiring social prestige:

> As I am using the term here, it is a quality a person has; a quality that is conferred upon him by others by virtue of his attributes, actions, competence, comportment and the like. It is not, of course, a finite quantity; one can have more or less of it; one can acquire some or lose a bit through performance or circumstances. In this definition, prestige adheres to the individual as a result of the evaluations made by the community, by his public; it does not inhere in the qualities or acts themselves. It is something the individual seeks, for having prestige conferred upon him serves his self-esteem, satisfies that need for positive affect that I see as so central an element in human sociality. (Goldschmidt 1990, 31–32)

This need for prestige is universal, though the qualities or actions that are awarded prestige vary from one culture to another or may vary in the same culture through time — in effect, it varies with cultural values. Individuals are also unequal in their talents, opportunities, and commitments; hence the need for affection produces further social differentiation and inequality, but it is this need for affection that is behind an individual's compliance with sociocultural needs and demands. It is also the cohesive glue that keeps the individual committed to the community or subculture with which she shares her values.

Finally, Goldschmidt introduces the concept of "career" to keep the focus on the individual as a motivated actor in the sociocultural system: "The individual career is the lifetime pursuit of satisfactions, both physical and social. The central feature of a career is a person's contribution to the production, protection and reproduction necessary for the community's continued existence, but it includes other valued activities that help to define the self in the context of the existing social order" (Goldschmidt 1990, 3).

Sociocultural materialism as a theory agrees with Karl Marx's statement that, "It is not the consciousness of men that determines their existence, but their social existence that determines their consciousness" (Marx 1859). The entire sociocultural system rests on the way society exploits its environment to meet the biological and psychological needs of its population. Because all humans share these needs, sociocultural systems can be interpreted as having universal organizing principles.

THE UNIVERSAL ORGANIZATION OF SOCIOCULTURAL SYSTEMS

Taking my cue from Harris (1979), there is a universal organization in sociocultural systems. Table 1.1 outlines the major components of sociocultural systems — the universal organization of human societies. It is termed *universal* because all societies, from hunting-and-gathering through industrial, are organized along the same lines. The table reflects a significant departure from Harris's theory to encompass advanced industrial societies better. These changes, however, do not violate Harris's universality—the theory can still be applied to any sociocultural system. What follows is a brief description of each component.

Infrastructure

Like all living organisms humans must obtain energy from their environment. The principal interface between a sociocultural system and its environment is the infrastructure. Infrastructure has two parts: the mode

TABLE 1.1
Revised Components of Sociocultural Systems

I. Environment
The physical, biological, and chemical restraints to which human action is subject

II. Infrastructure
- A. Mode of production: The technology and the practices employed for expanding or limiting basic subsistence production, especially the production of food and other forms of energy
  1. Technology of subsistence
  2. Techno-environmental relationships
  3. Work patterns
- B. Mode of reproduction: The technology and the practices employed for expanding, limiting, and maintaining population size
  1. Demography
  2. Mating patterns
  3. Fertility, natality, mortality
  4. Nurturance of infants
  5. Medical control of demographic patterns
  6. Contraception, abortion, infanticide

III. Structure
- A. Primary group structure: A small number of people who interact on an intimate basis and perform many functions, such as regulating reproduction, basic production, socialization, education, and enforcing domestic discipline. Examples:
  1. Family
  2. Community
  3. Voluntary organization
  4. Friendship networks
- B. Secondary group structure: These groups may be large or small, but their members tend to interact without any emotional commitment to one another. These organizations are coordinated through bureaucracies. They perform many functions, such as regulating production, reproduction, socialization, education, and enforcing social discipline. Hierarchies based on class, sex, race, caste, age, ethnic, and other statuses exist throughout the structure of society. Examples:
  1. Governments, parties, factions, military, police
  2. Corporations, businesses, industries
  3. Education, media, and other formal socialization agents
  4. Service and welfare organizations
  5. Professional and labor organizations

Table 1.1, continued

IV. Superstructure
- A. Cultural Superstructure
  1. Art, music, dance, literature, advertising
  2. Rituals
  3. Sports, games, hobbies
  4. Science
- B. Mental Superstructure: Conscious and unconscious motives for human behavior
  1. Values
  2. Emotions
  3. Traditions
  4. Zweckrationale (goal-oriented rational action)

Major Principle: Infrastructural determinism is the mode of production and reproduction, which determines primary and secondary group structure, which, in turn, determines the behavioral and mental superstructure.

Source: Adapted from Marvin Harris, 1979, pp. 46–76.

of production, which consists of behaviors that satisfy requirements for subsistence; and the mode of reproduction, which consists of behaviors that avoid destructive increases or decreases in population size. The modes of production and reproduction are attempts to strike a balance between reproduction and the consumption of energy from a finite environment. It is upon this infrastructural foundation that the remaining parts of the social system are based.

To illustrate the centrality of infrastructure, suppose we are members of a hunting-and-gathering band that has recently experienced some bad times, and we are experiencing food shortages. Looking at Table 1.1, what can we do with our infrastructure? When I ask my students this question I invariably receive two immediate responses: We can move to a new area that provides more food resources, or we can begin to plant seeds and raise animals to eat. Such answers are indicative of the modern sensibilities of industrial people, but they fail to acknowledge the tremendous hold of tradition and the value of place over the way of life of preindustrial people. Also, these solutions imply that new lands or new technologies are readily available. Hunting-and-gathering societies lasted millions of years. What infrastructural practices did they use to adapt to the limits of their natural environment?

The answer, of course, is through practices that were aimed at limiting population size. Despite the natural fecundity of women, population size remained stable for thousands of years; population growth was almost nonexistent. Preindustrial societies kept their numbers in check through a variety of social practices. According to Harris (1977, 11–25) these included such practices as infanticide (estimates are as high as 50 percent in some societies), geronticide, prolonged lactation (a technique that allows for the spacing of infants in women whose diets are close to minimal requirements), mating patterns (any change in mating patterns that would serve to reduce the birthrate, such as social approval of nonprocreative sex or delaying marriage), and other methods of population control.

Another possible avenue of fitting into an environment is through intensifying the mode of production, that is, devising new technologies and social practices to harvest more food from the environment. The two mechanisms of balancing between the material needs of a society and the environment — production and reproduction — are so essential for life that widespread practices and beliefs in the rest of the sociocultural system must be consistent with these practices. This is the "principle of infrastructural determinism," a process that drives the sociocultural evolutionary process — a process that will be more fully described in this chapter when we describe the dynamics of the system.

Structure

The structural components of sociocultural systems arise from the necessity of maintaining secure, predictable, and orderly relationships among individuals. The threat of disorder arises primarily from the allocation of labor and the distribution of goods and services to individuals and groups. Social organization regulates the allocation and distribution process. Although human organizations exist on a continuum, social structure can be divided into primary and secondary groups. Primary groups consist of small groups, such as the family, which regulates production, reproduction, exchange, and consumption in domestic settings. Secondary organizations are more impersonal groups such as government and industry, which regulate production, reproduction, exchange, and consumption within and among groups and sociocultural systems.

The primary-secondary dichotomy encompasses all human organizations that are responsible for the allocation and distribution of all biological and psychological need satisfaction. Primary groups tend to be informal and dominate the structures of traditional societies. They often are organized around kinship ties, and they regulate the activities of their members through informal norms and folkways of the culture. Secondary organizations are more formal and are usually coordinated through bureaucracy.

In order to study secondary organizations, in both historical and contemporary societies, Max Weber (1921) developed an "ideal-type" bureaucracy, which provides one of the basic methods for historical-comparative study. There can be an ideal-type whorehouse, religious sect, dictatorship, or democracy (none of which may be ideal in the usual sense of the term). According to Weber, bureaucracies are goal-oriented organizations that are set up according to rational principles, which are designed to efficiently attain organizational goals. Offices within a bureaucracy are ranked in a hierarchy. Information flows up the chain of command, directives flow down the chain. Operations of the organization are characterized by impersonal rules that explicitly state duties, responsibilities, procedures, authority, and conduct of the officeholders. The division of labor is highly specialized; appointments to these offices are made according to specialized qualifications rather than to ascribed characteristics; promotions and other rewards are given for achievement. All of these "ideal" characteristics have one goal — to promote the efficient attainment of the organization's goal, whether it is to produce cars, educate students, or administer social benefits. The characteristics of an ideal-type bureaucracy can be summarized as:

hierarchy;
impersonality;
written rules of conduct;
employment based on achieved characteristics such as education and motivation rather than ascribed characteristics such as race, relationship, or gender;
individual promotion based on achievement;
specialized division of labor; and
efficiency in the attainment of organizational goals.

Weber was well aware that the ideal type never corresponds to reality. It involves describing the logically consistent features of a social institution with which we can compare reality. All bureaucracies deviate from their ideal — there are many human factors that go into a university's decision to grant or deny tenure, for example, but the goal of a bureaucracy is to minimize these human factors (factors that do not contribute to the efficiency of the organization, or may even hinder the attainment of organization goals) through the further refinement of written rules and procedures. A bureaucracy is not considered static — it is constantly reevaluating its rules and procedures and engaging in an ever more refined division of labor to ensure greater efficiency in the attainment of its goals. Weber developed the ideal type to more accurately describe the growth in the power and scope of a bureaucracy in the modern world, and his studies of bureaucracy still form the core of organizational sociology.

The bureaucratic coordination of the action of large numbers of people has become the dominant structural feature of modern societies. It is only through this organizational device that large-scale planning and coordination, both for the modern state and economy, become possible. The consequence of the growth in the power and scope of these organizations is key to understanding our world.

Superstructure

The third component of sociocultural systems is the cultural superstructure. The term "culture" in sociology and anthropology refers to the values, norms, traditions, and material goods that characterize a group. Goldschmidt wrote of the origins of culture: "As interdependency increased, as sociality became more important, as communication became increasingly an essential ingredient of this sociality, a threshold was passed into language, into a systematic treatment of information. An unanticipated consequence of this evolutionary development was the creation of a symbolic world: a shared perception of the reality within which the community existed. In this symbolic world the individual is no longer merely a biological entity but is also a social entity. The self was born" (Goldschmidt 1990, 2–3). In line with Goldschmidt, my focus is on culture as a symbolic world of (mostly) shared perceptions of reality of a particular group. Although culture exists within the minds of individuals, it is the product of consensus, and it changes in the process of social interaction. Human individuals exist within both a physical and symbolic world. They are motivated to satisfy both their biological and psychological needs. Physical needs can be satisfied by a person's contribution to production and reproduction, which are necessary for the community. The psychological need for affection (or social honor) can be satisfied symbolically by engaging in these and other activities, which are valued by the existing social order.

Harris divided the superstructure along two lines. The behavioral superstructure consists of such activities as art, dance, literature, rituals, sports, and games. The mental superstructure consists of the conscious and unconscious goals, values, rules, philosophies, and beliefs that guide human behavior as they satisfy their biological and psychological needs. In this category Harris listed such diverse components as magic, religion, taboos, subsistence lore, ideologies, myths, aesthetic standards, and philosophies. Although Harris explicitly stated that these elements interact with structural and infrastructural parts of the social system, the thrust of his anthropology is on explaining these cultural elements in terms of ecological-infrastructural relationships.

The current focus, however, is on the systemic character of sociocultural systems. For this purpose it is useful to conceptualize the mental superstructure as a typology of human motivation. Weber (1921, 1–2) based his sociology on individuals as motivated actors in sociocultural systems. He identified four such motivators (or ideal types) of social action: zweckrational, or rational action in relation to a goal; wertrational, or rational action in relation to a value; affective or emotional action; and traditional action, which is dictated by custom or habit.

Zweckrational can be roughly translated as "technocratic thinking." It can be defined as actions in which the means to attain a particular goal are rationally chosen. An engineer who builds a bridge as the most efficient way to cross a river often exemplifies it in the literature. Perhaps a more relevant example is the modern goal of material success that is sought after by many people today. Many recognize that the most efficient way to attain success is through higher education, and so they flock to universities in order to get a good job.

Wertrational, or value-oriented rationality, is characterized by striving for a goal, which, in itself, may not be rational but which is pursued through rational means. The values come from within an ethical, religious, philosophical, or even holistic context — they are not rationally "chosen." The usual example in the literature is of an individual who seeks salvation by following the teachings of a prophet. A more relevant example is a person who attends university because he or she values the life of the mind — a value that was instilled by parents, previous teachers, or chance encounters.

Affective action is anchored in the emotional state of the person rather than the rational weighing of means and ends. Sentiments are powerful forces in motivating human behavior. Attending university for the community life of a fraternity, or following one's girlfriend to school are examples.

Traditional action is guided by customary habits of thought, by reliance on what Weber called "the eternal yesterday." Many students attend university because it is traditional for their social class and family to attend — the expectation was always there, it was never questioned.

Weber's typology is intended to be a comprehensive list of the types of meaning that men and women give to their conduct across sociocultural systems. As an advocate of multiple causation of human behavior, Weber was well aware that most behavior is caused by a mix of these motivations — university students, even today, have a variety of reasons for attending college. In marketing themselves to students, universities attempt to address (and encourage) all kinds of motivations. (A review of some university brochures, however, indicates a clear attempt to focus their appeal on goal-oriented rationality, or the career aspirations of the potential student. In addition, there is a marked tendency to portray many college classes as taking place in pastoral settings.)

However, Weber went further than a mere classification scheme. He developed the typology because he was primarily concerned with modern society and how it differs from societies of the past. He proposed that the basic distinguishing feature of modern society was a characteristic shift in the motivation of individuals. His classification of types of action provides a basis for his investigation of the social evolutionary process in which behavior had come to be increasingly dominated by goal-oriented rationality (zweckrational). He believed that more and more of our behaviors were being guided by zweckrational and less and less by tradition, values, or emotions. Because of this focus, he is often thought of as an "idealist" — one who believes that ideas and beliefs mold social structure and other material conditions — but Weber committed himself to no such narrow interpretation of sociocultural causation. He believed that this shift in human motivation is one of both cause and effect occurring in interaction with changes in the structural organization of society. The major thrust of Weber's works attempts to identify the factors that have brought about this "rationalization" of the West.

DYNAMICS OF SOCIOCULTURAL SYSTEMS

Figure 1.1 is a diagram of the sociocultural evolutionary process. I present it here because I think it neatly summarizes the structure and dynamics of sociocultural systems as discussed in this book. The universal organizational components are represented by boxes — the infrastructure, structure, and superstructure — all rooted on the bottom curved line that represents the environment. Just as there is a universal organization of sociocultural systems, so too are there universal dynamics of these systems.

FIGURE 1.1
Structure and Dynamics of Sociocultural Systems

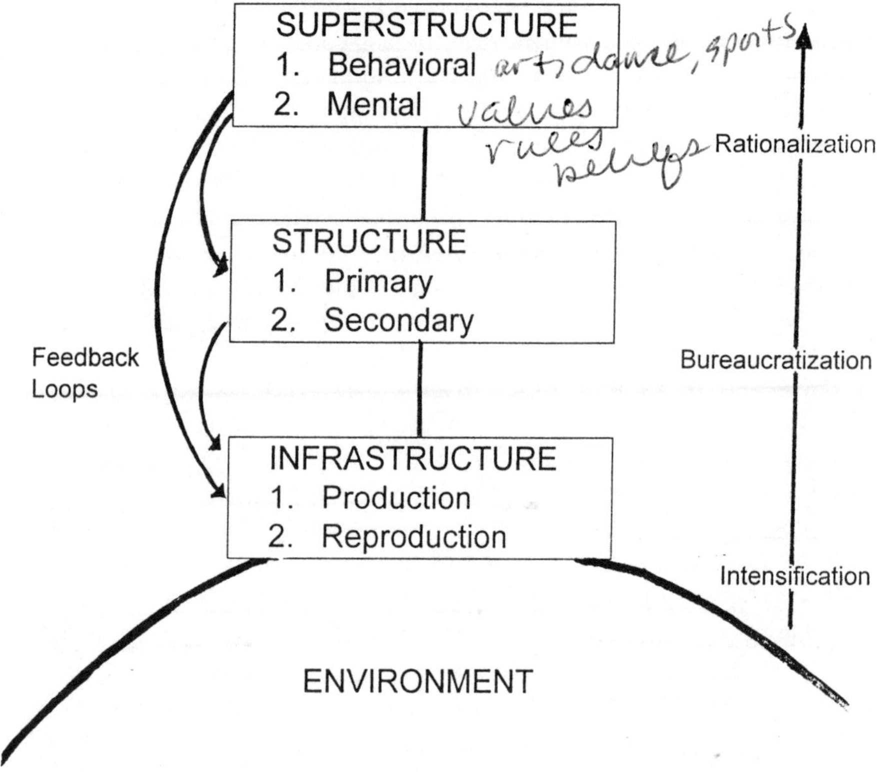

The dynamics of the social system are represented by the arrows on the right and left of the organizational boxes. Social change is depicted as beginning with the intensification process that is rooted in a society's relationship to its environment. As the population grows technology becomes more complex in order to secure the needed resources. The division of labor — that is, greater specialization to increase production — becomes more pronounced. As productivity rises so does population, spurring further intensification of production. This intensification process profoundly influences social organization. In a society with a diverse and growing division of labor, complicated production techniques, and a population running into the millions the traditional organization and coordination of societies begins to break down. Primary groups, such as the family and community, lose many of their traditional roles, such as coordinating production (farms, small shops), educating the young, teaching trades and crafts, caring for the old and sick, and providing political protection. Secondary organizations — often coordinated by bureaucracies that are designed specifically to provide this coordination — proliferate, enlarge, and centralize.

This bureaucratization of structure (as well as the intensification of infrastructure) encourages the rationalization process — the increasing dominance of logic, observation, and reason in guiding human behavior (as opposed to tradition, values, and emotions). The arrows on the left of the diagram represent system feedback loops. The increasing dominance of technocratic thinking among industrial peoples becomes a habit of thought, a way of perceiving the world. When confronted with problems of human organization or problems in securing food or other vital resources from a depleting environment, industrial people apply these rational principles to solve these problems, often with little thought to tradition or the consequences of their action on the social whole. Both public and private bureaucracy, of course, encourage the intensification process. It is, indeed, a system with the various parts of that system in interaction with one another.

Although cultural materialism rejects the value-laden notion of progress, it is an evolutionary theory. Productive and reproductive forces have expanded throughout history (especially in the last 200 years). Great transitions in human societies are an outgrowth of the intensification process — transitions that involve a shift in the mode of production from, say, hunting-and-gathering to production based on horticulture. The intensification of infrastructures inevitably leads to environmental depletion, which results in either the sudden collapse of a sociocultural system (which happened to the inhabitants of Easter Island, for example) or a shift to a new mode of production. If a culture successfully shifts to a new mode of production, the intensification process begins again.

Throughout history, the intensification of production has always been toward greater complexity because the process leads to the exploitation of less available, harder-to-reach sources of energy (we always use the easily exploited resources first). Similarly, when critical resources are depleted, the shift to a new mode of production represents a move from a readily available source of energy (wood, for example) to a less accessible source (coal, oil, or nuclear fission, for example). Over the course of social evolution mankind has had to engage in more complicated processing and production techniques in order to draw energy from the environment. We will return to intensification and the environment in Chapter 2, "Sociocultural Evolution," when we examine the relationship between the environment and the intensification process to general sociocultural change.

Bureaucratization of Structure

As early as 1885, Herbert Spencer associated the growth of bureaucracy directly with greater diversity of interests caused by the growth of population and the division of labor. Greater numbers of people, Spencer argued, require rational social organization to coordinate and regulate their diverse activities. The world has experienced exponential growth in population over the last two centuries. As population has increased, formal organizations have developed to solve problems of adapting to the environment (government and corporation), handling survival needs (sanitation and food production), and providing social services (welfare and medical care). In addition, according to Spencer, the division of labor makes society more fragile and subject to disruption. Regulating centers (bureaucratic administration) are necessary to coordinate the diverse activities and interests in such a society — in Spencer's terms, "supreme regulating centers and subordinate ones" (Spencer 1885, 46).

Robert Michels also related the growing division of labor directly with bureaucratic growth. "The principle of division of labor coming more and more into operation, executive authority undergoes division and subdivision. There is thus constituted a rigorously defined and hierarchical bureaucracy" (Michels 1915, 72). Hierarchies based on class, sex, race, and other statuses exist throughout all sociocultural systems. This is not to say that the elites in hierarchies always rule in the manner of divine-right kings. The amount of power and control exercised by elites varies across societies and through time; however, there exists within every society dominant elites who possess a disproportionate amount of social power. They are able to impose direct economic and political sanctions to buttress their position. In addition, they are able to mobilize superstructural support by indirectly encouraging ideas and ideologies that are favorable to their interests. A sociocultural materialist analysis attempts to identify the elites; gauge the amount of power they wield; and uncover their biases, assumptions, and interests.

The biopsychological well-being of those at the top of the sex, age, class, race, caste, or ethnic hierarchies of society will weigh more heavily than the well-being of those at the bottom. Changes that enhance the position of elites are likely to be amplified and propagated throughout the entire sociocultural system. Changes that undermine these positions will be fiercely resisted. Chapter 3, "Structures of Authority," details the growth in the size and scope of bureaucratic power in modern industrial society. In that chapter we will examine both the nature of this power and the elite interests that are being served by further industrialization and bureaucratization.

The growth of mass production, the increasing interdependence of economic activity (globalization), and the consequent increase in job specialization have led to greater needs for coordination of these diverse activities. A modern automobile-manufacturing corporation, for example, must coördinate the activities of thousands of employees, suppliers, and dealers around the globe. More complex technologies and markets require rational social organization to coordinate, control, and regulate these activities. One of the fundamental reasons behind the emergence and growth of bureaucracies is that they enable large-scale tasks to be performed. In Chapter 4, "Economic Rationalization," we will examine how recent intensification and the resulting bureaucratization of the economy have caused the growth in the power of corporations, financial institutions, and governments around the world. We will then turn to how these changes have affected our work life — one of our most fundamental ways of relating to one another.

A further factor behind the growth of bureaucracies is the decline in the size, influence, and importance of primary-group organization. Industrial societies require a mobile population. People must move from one end of a country to the other in order to engage in their occupations. Bureaucratic-industrial societies require social mobility as well. This weakens many traditional groups such as the family and the community. In traditional societies, the family and community provide many services to the individual — child care, social security, financial aid, education, medical care, counseling, and other services. With the decline of primary groups, many secondary organizations have arisen in industrial societies to provide the services that used to be performed by traditional groups.

The rise of bureaucracy, then, is in large part an effort to deal with the breakdown of traditional ways of organizing social life. What the family, community, ethnic groups, friendship network, and church once did, private corporations and government now attempt to do. Whereas traditional groups provided aid and services on the basis of ties of affection and tradition, bureaucracies provide aid and services through contractual-legal relationships and self-interest. The traditional ways broke down because of infrastructural intensification. In Chapter 5, "Erosion of Commitment," we will examine the impact of industrialization and the growing division of labor on the family and the community — again, two fundamental institutions through which we bond with one another and with the culture as a whole. In Chapter 6, "Factual Regularities," and Chapter 7, "Widening Gyre," we will examine the impact of bureaucratization and rationalization on some traditional forms of social life — specifically, health care, agriculture, higher education, and politics. In each case, I believe, it will be shown that fundamental infrastructural intensification has affected areas far removed from simple economic life.

Rationalization

The rationalization process is the practical application of knowledge to achieve a desired end. It leads to efficiency, coordination, and control over both the physical and social environment and is the guiding principle behind bureaucracy and the increasing division of labor. It has led to an unprecedented increase in both the production and distribution of goods and services. It is also associated with secularization, depersonalization, and oppressive routine. As the industrial mode of production intensifies, the rationalization of social life continues apace. Human behavior is increasingly guided by observation, experiment, and reason (zweckrational) to master the natural and social environment to achieve a desired end.

Perhaps the most obvious examples of the rationalization process concern the reinterpretation of Christian religious beliefs, values, traditions, and practices that are in conflict with advanced industrial society. The examples are legion. Traditional Christianity, for example, held to the tradition of Sunday as a day of rest. The way I remember it, unless one had an ox that was in need of immediate rescue (falling into a pit comes to mind), one was supposed to take Sunday as a day of rest and reflection. Apparently, many oxen have fallen into pits in recent years. In 1950s America, most businesses — including grocery stores — were closed on Sundays (this is still the case in many countries — often because of law). By the 1970s, the picture had changed dramatically. Grocery stores and commercial stores of all types are now open for business on Sundays.

Another example is the Christian prohibition against lending money. The early church originally banned the practice of lending money — one of the key activities of capitalism. In the Middle Ages the practice of lending money became the province of Jews. Over the centuries, however, the tradition has been reinterpreted. First, the prohibition was said to be one of charging interest, then, one of usury (a particularly useful interpretation because the usury criterion could float with the prevailing loan rate of the economy). Now the prohibition is generally ignored (which should be comforting to banks that issue credit cards).

Still other examples concern the conflict of religion and science. The Church originally held the Bible to be authoritative in matters of nature. When Galileo threw in his lot with Copernicus, the Church forced him to recant. Over the centuries, as the scientific world view has gained strength in evidence and allegiance, the Church has had to reinterpret its views — recently admitting, for example, that it was in error in bringing Galileo to trial as well as stating even more recently that natural evolution was not inconsistent with Catholicism. Many Protestant sects, however, have continued the latter conflict in America by holding to creationism. It is interesting that with the development of "creation science," many creationists have attempted to redefine the conflict from one of religion-versus-science to one of competing "scientific" theories (an interpretation that was not upheld by the Supreme Court). This is an excellent example of rationalization in both the sociological sense and the popular sense.

It is interesting to interpret the current conflict between Christian traditions and values and modern views and values as one of rationalization. The Catholic Church, for example, is between the proverbial rock and hard place on many social issues. On the one hand, many of its traditions, such as not allowing women in the priesthood, celibacy among priests, and its ban on all forms of birth control, are clearly out of step with modernity. On the other hand, tradition and values are part of the bedrock of Catholicism itself. Should it bow to reform, it will lose many of its traditional followers (as it did as a result of the Vatican II Council in the 1960s). If it continues to resist, it will continue to lose many of its younger (and more "rationalized") followers. Mainstream Protestant churches in America have, in large part, bowed to the forces of modernity and have lost followers (and believers) as a result. Worse, many of the leaders (and followers) in Protestant churches have lost the core faith in the divinity of Christ. True believers now flock to the more traditional churches of Pentecostal (emotionally based) and fundamentalist (traditionally based) Protestantism.

The rationalization of superstructure is the increasing dominance of a mode of thought that involves a persistent questioning of the adequacy of means to ends and a constant search for more adequate means. The result is a society that questions traditional ways and devises more rational ways to achieve its desired ends. The rationalization of superstructure provides positive feedback for further bureaucratization of structure, both of which provide positive feedback for the further intensification process.

Feedback Loops

Although the infrastructure is considered to be of primary importance, the structure and superstructure are not mere reflections of infrastructural processes but are in interaction with these processes. Society is a very stable system. The most likely outcome of any change in the system — whether this change begins in the infrastructure, structure, or superstructure — is resistance in other sectors of the system. This system-maintaining negative feedback is capable of dampening or extinguishing most system change. The result is either the extinction of the innovation or slight compensatory changes that preserve the fundamental character of the whole system.

An example of a structural change that received a lot of negative feedback was the commune movement of the 1960s. At the time, many social scientists were predicting that the commune represented a real alternative lifestyle. There were predictions that, in the future, we would all have to struggle with the choice of either starting a traditional family or joining a commune, but the commune met with harsh resistance (and sanctions) from existing institutions (family, church, local government), ideologies, and traditions (monogamy, Christianity). In addition, like the extended family before it, a commune does not allow for easy geographic or social mobility of its members. As a result, few of our young are now struggling with the choice.

Not every change, however, that meets resistance in the structure, superstructure, or both, is extinguished. Women who worked outside the home, a change caused by the rising cost of living and a declining birth rate (both infrastructural changes), encountered fierce resistance from traditional families, many secondary organizations (corporations, unions, churches, government), and superstructures (Christianity, ideology, traditions, and beliefs). Despite this opposition, American society is currently adjusting its institutions and ideologies to accommodate the change.

Weber's general theory of rationalization (of which bureaucratization is but a particular case) refers to increasing human mastery over the natural and social environment. In truth, the intensification of the infrastructure is nothing more than the application of goal-oriented rational behavior to regulate the flow of energy from the environment. The increasing application of the method and substance of science in the structure parallels this intensification of infrastructure: more complex technologies and greater numbers of people require rational social organization for coordination and control. The intensification of the infrastructure leads to the growth of secondary organizations at the expense of primary groups. In turn, these changes in social structure have changed human character by changing values, philosophies, and beliefs in the superstructure of society. The bureaucratization process has encouraged such superstructural norms and values as individualism, efficiency, self-discipline, materialism, and calculability (all of which are subsumed under Weber's concept of zweckrational). These goals and values then provide positive feedback for further bureaucratization and intensification. Both rationalization and bureaucratization then provide positive feedback for the further intensification process. This feedback is crucial in understanding the character of system change.

In Chapter 8, "New Ideology," we will examine the ideology of postindustrialism, an ideology that directly encourages further infrastructural growth. This ideology serves to celebrate technological change; to explain away the growth of private and public bureaucratic power; and to obscure the decline of community, traditional family, and personal control over our actions in the workplace. It is the old idea of progress in a high-tech bottle.

I have made every effort in this book to outline this system-like character — intensification, bureaucratization, rationalization, and feedback — in describing various parts of sociocultural systems. The concluding chapter, "Possibilities," explicitly examines the systemic character of society and the environmental-social constraints on future sociocultural evolution.

CONCLUSIONS

I stress the systemic character of sociocultural materialism. The theoretical synthesis is, of course, from a variety of classical and contemporary social theorists. I began with the work of Marvin Harris, who was profoundly influenced by Marx and Malthus. I have modified this basic theory in order to integrate the insights of a variety of classical sociologists. Specifically, I have abandoned Harris's structural concepts and substituted the sociological dichotomy of primary and secondary group structures and incorporated the Weberian concept of human action into Harris's concept of superstructure. I did this for a number of reasons.

First, as a cultural anthropologist, Harris is very concerned with describing and explaining sociocultural practices and beliefs. In other words, his focus is almost exclusively on structures and superstructures as dependent variables that can be explained by infrastructural processes. Although Harris frequently argues that structures and superstructures interact with infrastructural processes, his theory has a difficult time generalizing these interactions. The modifications I make to Harris's posited structure and superstructure will allow a much stronger emphasis on structural and superstructural feedback in determining sociocultural stability and change. This, I believe, is essential in attempting to capture the systemic character of sociocultural systems.

Second, the primary-secondary group dichotomy is relatively simple to grasp (Harris's structural dichotomy is not), and it is comprehensive in describing two basic types of structures in human societies. I have substituted Weber's typology of motivators of human action for Harris's concept of superstructure for similar reasons. The typology represents an inclusive list that cuts across all sociocultural systems; it is thus more powerful in describing relationships between the various components of the social system.

Third, the synthesis of the primary-secondary typology and Weber's theory of action into sociocultural materialism enables it to encompass one of the fundamental evolutionary processes in human societies. This shift has been variously described as a movement from mechanical to organic solidarity (Emile Durkheim), Gemeinschaft to Gesellschaft (Ferdinand Tönnies), increasing complexity of structure (Herbert Spencer), and the increasing division of labor (almost all sociologists). Weber generalized this important evolutionary trend as the growth of rationalization, which has been discussed in this chapter; I believe his general theory of increasing rationalization is one of the most powerful tools we have for understanding modern sociocultural systems.

Finally, by synthesizing Weber's concepts and theory into the structure and superstructure — without doing violence to Harris's basic ecological theory — cultural materialism is greatly strengthened. In practical terms, the theory is now better equipped to deal with the most pressing problems of our time — growing inequality within and between nations, the destruction of community, growing dehumanization, environmental degradation — all of which must be understood in the context of the entire sociocultural system. In theoretical terms, it is a synthesis that can better integrate diverse, middle-range theories and empirical findings, a theory that can provide direction to our empirical studies, and a framework for our students to better understand the social world.

In effect, this book is an exploration of modern industrial societies according to a sociocultural materialist analysis. How suited is the theory in making our social life comprehensible? Is the theory a useful symbolic guide for understanding both the stability and change of our social world? This is the major task and promise of the social studies disciplines.

2

Sociocultural Evolution

The ancient Greeks thought that societies passed through stages. Beginning with a Golden Age, each succeeding age (Silver, Brass, Heroic, and Iron) passed through successive stages, and each stage was seen as harsher and more degraded than the previous one. Until the industrial revolution, many Western scholars viewed sociocultural change as leading humankind away from the ideal social order of antiquity (the Garden of Eden is a view of similar type). Such a world view led many people to consider their era as cruel and harsh, the future as worse still. It was not until the end of the seventeenth century that the modern idea of progress was born. Early sociologists were profoundly influenced by the idea of progress, linking their analysis of fundamental change under the assault of industrialism to theories about the direction of those changes.

Contrary to popular belief, the concept of evolution was not simply borrowed from biology. Rather, it seems theories of social and biological evolution developed along parallel lines in the nineteenth century, at times influencing one another (Carneiro 1967, x). Many evolutionary theorists, both social and biological, used the terms "evolution" and "progress" interchangeably. For many thinkers in the nineteenth century, social evolution was linked to change that would gradually lead to the ultimate triumph of some principle or condition. Social theorists identified such principles and conditions as equality, material wealth, freedom, or reason as the ultimate "goal" of accumulating social change. (Many biological theorists had a similar fixation on ultimate "directions" of evolution, positing that the evolution of intelligent life was such a goal.)

The close identification of progress and social evolution has led to evolution's decline in modern social thought. Sociologists first became disenchanted with the idea of progress and then hostile to seemingly unilinear theories that posited social change in all societies in a common direction (Carneiro 1967, iii). Social evolution fell out of fashion and, until recently, has been almost totally ignored by modern-day sociologists.

Sociocultural materialism is an avowedly evolutionary perspective. A synthesis of theories of broad scope, sociocultural materialism results in a body of theory that cuts across historical eras to explain the origin, maintenance, and change of sociocultural systems. At its base, there is an insistence on the centrality of infrastructural-environmental relationships in explaining sociocultural change, but this insistence in no way negates the importance of structures and cultural beliefs in the evolutionary process. The evolutionary process can only be fully accounted for by reference to the interaction of environmental, demographic, and technological factors with social structures and cultural superstructures.

The evolutionary process can be briefly summarized as follows: Social practices and institutions change in response to the availability of natural resources upon which a society depends for survival. The environment changes through both natural processes (the character of sociocultural and environmental interaction makes the term "natural" increasingly difficult to define) and through the impact of the activities of men and women in pursuit of their biological and psychological needs. Successful social changes are those that promote the exploitation of more energy and raw materials (particularly food) from the environment. Sociocultural systems are susceptible to the lure of such changes because our ability to reproduce has always been greater than our ability to find food for our children's survival (Harris 1979). All widespread social practices and beliefs must be compatible with the way society goes about exploiting its environment, because these practices are necessary for life itself.

Successful sociocultural changes are institutionalized in our structure and preserved in the culture. They are handed down to our children through the socialization process. In addition, sociocultural systems "learn" from one another through social contact and conquest. The evolutionary process is one of sociocultural systems, each with its own unique history, in interaction with their natural and social environment.

In this chapter I will briefly present the evidence for the importance of infrastructural-environmental relationships interacting with structural and cultural elements of the sociocultural system to explain the two great transitions in human societies: first, the move from hunting-and-gathering societies to those based on horticulture, and second, the transition from agrarian production to industrialism. Both of these transitions involved a qualitative change (or a change in kind) in the mode of production; both involved a change in the resources upon which the sociocultural system relied for its energy needs. Finally, both revolutionized social life. These great transitions in human societies, it will be demonstrated, were a direct outgrowth of the intensification process. Then, we will turn to the general characteristics of sociocultural evolution and finish with a discussion of how our past evolution affects the way we see the social world.

NEOLITHIC REVOLUTION

The Neolithic Revolution refers to the transition from hunting-and-gathering societies to horticulture societies. Horticulture is a far more productive and stable means of production than hunting and gathering is. Until recently, many anthropologists saw its adoption as a natural outgrowth of the accumulation of cultural information. The problem with this view is that some evidence suggests that hunters and gatherers often knew about the relationship between seeds and plants. Although some horticultural techniques were occasionally used to supplement hunting and gathering for thousands of years, intensive horticulture did not "naturally" follow. As with all preindustrial people, the hold of tradition was great. Hunters and gatherers placed a great value on their way of life and did not give it up unless they were forced to do so (Lenski 1966; Lenski, Nolan, & Lenski 1995).

In 1977, Marvin Harris pointed out that any adequate explanation of the transition must account for two findings of archeology. First, the explanation must detail why so many of the world's people chose to domesticate plants and animals after millions of years of subsistence through hunting and gathering during one brief span of time — between 10,000 and 2,000 B.C. Second, the explanation must account for how the transition took place independently (that is, without any social contact) in different parts of the world. These two factors place some constraints on social theory. To posit that a great man or woman had an idea becomes problematic. The first problem is one of timing — the knowledge base for horticulture appears to have existed long before it was adopted. Second, several great ideas would have had to arise independently in many societies, and geniuses would have had to be born in a very brief span of years. To be plausible, Harris stated, any theory of the transition from hunting and gathering to the domestication of plants and animals must be a theory of process, not of singular events.

Mark Cohen attempted to explain why so many of the world's people chose to domesticate plants and animals over hunting-and-gathering. Cohen's theory is one of process. He asserts that the transition was made because of changes in the natural environment, specifically, the onset of the interglacial period about 13,000 years ago. The receding of the glaciers was an event that took place over generations. Global warming greatly changed climates; it caused a diversity of effects in different regions of the world. The global scale of this event caused the simultaneous emergence (within 6 thousand years) of different types of agricultural practices throughout the world. Differing environments led to the domestication of different plant and animal species — such as rice and soybeans in China and maize and squash in the Americas (also see Lenski 1966; and Lenski, Nolan, & Lenski 1995).

In northern Europe, as the glaciers began to recede, vast tundra, which had supported herds of mammoth, steppe bison, and other prey animals, began to be replaced by forests. The response by hunters and gatherers was to intensify their efforts. New technology was developed, such as the atala (spear thrower) and the bow and arrow, which allowed hunters to kill more prey (Lenski, Nolan, & Lenski 1995). This intensification solved immediate pressures but led to longer-term shortages. When people became more productive, more children survived infancy, which put a greater strain on a depleting environment. The intensification of social infrastructures — a process that Harris defined as the growth of human populations, greater expenditures of energy to secure food and resources from the environment, and increased productivity — was off and running. The loss of grazing lands, together with the increasing toll taken by humans, had a devastating effect on the resources that hunter-gatherers relied upon for subsistence. Many prey species became depleted or extinct, which led to further intensification efforts.

There was a gradual increase of human populations toward the end of the hunting-and-gathering era (Lenski, Nolan, & Lenski 1995, 121). As the labor costs of hunting and gathering rose and the benefits fell, alternative modes of production became more attractive. The transition, then, was out of necessity, rather than the simple result of the accumulation of knowledge or the appearance of a genius who had an idea. Accumulated knowledge did not result in agricultural development until the existing mode of production could no longer meet the biological and psychological needs of the population. Gradually, over generations, people began to supplement their hunting and gathering with the domestication of plants and animals. Many societies arrived at the practice through this process. Others learned it through contact or conquest. In time, the domestication of plants and animals became the primary productive strategy of most of the world's societies. Social structures and cultural superstructures were critical to determining the character and timing of the transition.

Social structures and superstructures also had to change dramatically in response to this infrastructural intensification. So great was this change that social scientists have come to refer to it as revolutionary — meaning the entire ways of life of societies were transformed. The horticultural way of life led to profoundly different governments, family structures, stratification systems, religious beliefs, and knowledge bases. Only one other social process in history rivals the profound changes of this period — the Industrial Revolution.

THE INDUSTRIAL REVOLUTION

The industrial revolution involved the transformation of technology based on human and animal labor to technology based on the use of inanimate energy sources: "the period during which the productive activities of societies were rapidly transformed by the invention of a succession of machines powered by newer, inanimate sources of energy, such as coal, electricity, petroleum, and natural gas" (Lenski, Nolan, & Lenski 1995, 225). Along with the industrial revolution came the transformation in employment from the vast majority of people working on the land (as many as 95 percent directly or indirectly) to employment in factories, shops, and service agencies. Whereas the industrial revolution was a revolution in technology, it created profound changes in social structures and superstructures. It brought new methods of agricultural production, new methods in the production and exchange of goods, and profound changes in the organization of labor. These changes, in turn, led to changes in community, family life, government, ideologies, and even ways of thought.

The term "Industrial Revolution" is really an arbitrary construct that stands for a very complex reality. The use of the term often leads us to treat it as a singular event when, in fact, the term is only an abstraction of an ongoing social process. There is no singular event that marked its beginning or ending except as defined by social consensus — it was not a thing but rather an abstraction that we use to break the continuous world of reality into a piece that we can manipulate. Like other forms of technology, these abstractions have a totalitarian character — they tend to simplify by arbitrarily leaving out complexity.

Many argue that the acceleration of industrial activity started well before the middle of the eighteenth century (the beginning date cited by most historians); some mark the beginning of the revolution in the middle of the sixteenth century or even earlier (Lenski, Nolan, & Lenski 1995, 225). Technological innovations (such seemingly simple devices as horse collars and three-field rotation) were producing food surpluses (and stimulating population growth) as early as the ninth century. However, most scholars mark the beginning of the industrial revolution with inventions such as the steam engine, the mechanization of textile production, and innovations and expansion in the iron industry — the technological changes that brought on the fundamental transformation to modern industrial forms. That is, we mark the initial phase as beginning in the middle of the eighteenth century (in line with the earlier definition by Lenski, Nolan, and Lenski). However, it is important to keep in mind that the industrial revolution was a gradually intensifying process of technological innovation that occurred over generations (and, I argue, is still ongoing), rather than a discreet event. We are seriously misleading ourselves by reifying the industrial revolution — that is, by considering the term as a concrete part of social reality rather than understanding the term as a construct that more or less arbitrarily labels a part of a continuous process of technological development.

Another difficulty in dealing with the causes of the industrial revolution is the sheer number of causes. The causes of the industrial revolution are many and varied. Books, dissertations, and papers have been devoted to the subject. The interaction of many sociocultural factors plays a role in social evolution. We are dealing with very complex systems — structures and superstructures — that provide important feedback to infrastructural change. In western Europe, these factors include such superstructural phenomena as Weber's *The Protestant Ethic and the Spirit of Capitalism* (1958) and the accumulation of technical and scientific knowledge; structural factors, such as the rise of capitalism and the division of political authority; infrastructural factors, such as population pressure and the availability of needed raw materials and energy; and unique historical circumstances, such as the discovery of the New World. Even Harris, who has often been accused of placing too much emphasis on infrastructural causation, assigns important roles to the structural development of capitalism and the superstructural techniques and products of science in causing the industrial revolution (Harris 1977). The full exploration of sociocultural system interactions makes for good sociology (and anthropology and history) but poor social theory. The goal of social theory is not to detail every conceivable relationship but to provide a concise world view that summarizes, orders, and weighs what appear to be the most important relationships among social phenomena.

As a research strategy and general method for understanding societies, sociocultural materialism directs us to first examine infrastructural-environmental relationships in our explanations of change in sociocultural systems, before examining structural and superstructural feedback in interaction with these changes. An adequate explanation of the initial industrial revolution must first address a twofold process: Why did England abandon the agrarian mode of production? Why did England increasingly turn to technologies powered by inanimate sources of energy?

The sociocultural materialist explanation begins with the intensification of the agrarian infrastructure. The soils of western Europe are heavy and moist, which makes traditional scratch plowing difficult. The cross plow, which was introduced widely in the ninth century, was equipped with a heavy blade to dig deep into the earth and a moldboard to turn over the soil. By bringing more nutrients to the surface for plant life, the cross plow greatly improved the productivity of the land. This increased productivity stimulated population growth. Increased population pressure created demands for increased crop yields. Agriculture began to further intensify. Such innovations as a three-field rotation system, clearing of more forests for cultivation, and draining of swamps all were put into practice to intensify agricultural production. From the first, the intensification of agriculture caused economic and demographic booms that would then run into environmental limits on resources that were unable to accommodate the growing population, which caused stagnation and decline. "The economy and population of Europe grew dramatically beginning in the ninth or tenth century, fed by a spectacular improvement in agriculture and trade. Environmental and economic reversals — most visibly the Black Death of the mid-fourteenth century, but also resources that were unable to accommodate a growing population — then led to a fourteenth century depression" (Gutmann 1988, 6). These cycles of economic and demographic boom followed by long periods of stagnation and decline characterize the infrastructures of western Europe up to the nineteenth century. These changes in the agrarian economy shaped the development of industry by affecting the availability of natural resources and manpower.

By the sixteenth century, landowners in England began enclosing common pasture land, raising sheep in vast numbers for the wool trade, and charging tenants money instead of accepting service or produce in order to maintain their living standards (Lenski, Nolan, & Lenski 1995, 223). When a new wave of inflation hit in the eighteenth century, landowners innovated by devising a system of crop rotation, which allowed continuous cultivation of fields (previously, fields would have to lie fallow for at least one year in four). Other innovations included the selective breeding of livestock to improve productivity and the invention of a variety of simple machines, which increased the efficiency of farm labor (Lenski, Nolan, & Lenski 1995, 223). "By the end of the eighteenth century, the traditional system of agriculture had been replaced in most of England by a new system of larger, more efficient farms operated on rational and capitalistic principles" (Lenski, Nolan, & Lenski 1995, 224). The adoption of this new system led to massive displacement of rural families as well as serious shortages of resources. Energy was the primary resource shortage that these societies faced. Thousands of square miles of timberland were cleared for commercial activity and brought under cultivation for growing food for an expanding population.

William McNeill addressed the medieval energy shortage directly: "Between about 1650 and 1750, western Europeans faced a growing crisis as a result of the rapid disappearance of forests. Timber, fuel, and rough pasturage traditionally had come from Europe's forests. But as more and more people put greater demands upon the forests, big trees became scarce" (McNeill 1993, 442). Wood is the primary natural resource in an agrarian society. Wood was used not only for energy but also as the primary raw material for making household utensils, wagons, looms, and other tools.

Wood was also the primary source of energy used in the growing commercial ventures of the production of iron, glass, and ships. "Up to the middle of the eighteenth century, the pecuniary and material limitations on the transport of charcoal or wood restricted growth and often compelled the ironmaster to halt work for as much as several months while sufficient fuel was collected for another run" (Landis 1969, 94). Shortages of wood created severe problems; they threatened a whole way of life. The crisis was especially acute in England. From the sixteenth century on, the need for new sources of energy in a country that had been almost denuded of its forests led to the substitution of coal for wood in a wide variety of industrial operations. "At the same time, the consumption of coal for domestic purposes rose steadily: there was perhaps a time, in the sixteenth century, when the Englishman recoiled at the acrid, sulphurous fumes of burning coal; but by the modern period, such scruples were laid by familiarity and necessity" (Landis 1969, 95–96). By 1700 in England, coal was rapidly replacing wood as the energy resource for both domestic use and for the growing commercial activities.

Landis also noted that the growth of industry was highly dependent upon the intensification of technology for the exploitation of coal. Coal was increasingly needed on a massive scale. "The development of mechanized industry concentrated in large units of production would have been impossible without a source of power greater than what human and animal strength could provide and independent of the vagaries of nature. The answer was found in a new converter of energy — the steam engine; and in the exploitation on a tremendous scale of an old fuel — coal. Each of these called the other forth. The strongest source of demand for increased power was mining, especially coal mining" (Landis 1969, 95). As coal mines had to be sunk deeper, they would go beneath the water table; water seeped into the shafts. Landis noted that this problem was so severe that some pits had to be abandoned; he describes one mine in Warwickshire where "five hundred horses were employed to hoist the water, bucket by bucket" (Landis 1969, 96).

Early in the eighteenth century, Thomas Savery and Thomas Newcome invented the atmospheric engine to pump the water out of the shafts (Landis 1969; Lenski, Nolan, & Lenski 1995). This engine laid the foundation for James Watt's invention of the first true steam engine later in the century. The steam engine was then quickly adapted to ventilate the mines, lift the coal out of the shafts, and transport the coal to markets. This is the meaning of Landis's phrase "each of these calls the other forth." In order to exploit reserves of coal more intensively, technology was developed to pump the water out of the mines. The steam engine (which converts the new energy source, coal, into mechanical energy), as well as the raw energy of the coal itself, was then used to intensify production in a host of other industries. Although many sociocultural factors must go into any full explanation of the industrial revolution, the fact that England was forced to change its resource base from wood to coal, and the technological innovations that had to be made to make that transition, must be accounted as prime movers.

GENERAL CHARACTERISTICS OF SOCIOCULTURAL EVOLUTION

There is an identifiable sociocultural evolutionary process. In this section I will summarize that process as identified by Harris in 1979 and Lenski, Nolan, and Lenski in 1995. Harris has been one of the strongest advocates of ecological-evolutionary theory in general and cultural materialism in particular. Gerhard Lenski, along with his coauthors Patrick Nolan and Jean Lenski, an anthropologist, have kept the ecological-evolutionary perspective alive in sociology. The two bodies of work have much in common. Both strongly advocate the centrality of infrastructural-environmental relationships in determining sociocultural evolution. Lenski, Nolan, and Lenski tend to put more emphasis on a society's social environment and on structural and superstructural feedback in general, but this is only a matter of emphasis, not really a difference in general theory. (Harris's critics are simply incorrect when they assert that he reduces all society to mere reflections of infrastructure.) The two perspectives are almost identical; both are in fundamental agreement with the following:

1. There is no preestablished direction to the social evolutionary process. Societies evolve in response to changes in their natural environment or as the result of contact with other societies.
2. Sociocultural systems evolve through the adaptations of individual behavior. "Just as a species does not 'struggle to survive' as a collective entity, but survives or not as a consequence of the adaptive changes of individual organisms, so too do sociocultural systems survive or not as a consequence of the adaptive changes in the thought and activities of individual men and women who respond opportunistically to cost-benefit options" (Harris 1979, 61).
3. Societies can be remarkably stable over time. Hunting-and-gathering societies existed with few technological, population, and structural changes for thousands of years. Ancient civilizations that depended upon river irrigation for food production were also remarkably stable. Both societies were successful at striking a balance between reproduction and the energy they consumed from their finite resources.
4. There was a biopsychological cost to maintaining this balance for preindustrial people. Our ability to produce children has always been greater than our ability to produce food for their survival. In order to limit population size preindustrial societies have always practiced infanticide and other forms of population control.
5. The hold of tradition was particularly strong among preindustrial peoples. Its power and hold over people has not been appreciated by observers in the twentieth century. It has been a great conservative force throughout social evolution (up to now at least).
6. The modes of production in human societies have, historically, intensified — that is, over time they have required more technical knowledge, skills, and nonhuman forms of energy. The intensification process exists because people must continually exploit less available, harder-to-reach sources of energy.

7. Similarly, if "absolute" environmental depletion is reached and a society has accumulated the technical knowledge to shift to a new mode of production, the shift is from a readily accessible source (wood, for example) to a less accessible source (such as coal, oil, or nuclear fission in its turn). Each succeeding energy source is more difficult to exploit. Each takes more general knowledge, capital, technology, and technical skill to tap.
8. The intensification of the modes of production has also greatly increased productivity. Although people must work harder to exploit each succeeding resource base, each new resource base represents a richer source of energy, which allows more food and other products to be produced.
9. Because preindustrial people kept their population in balance with their environment mainly through infanticide, increased wealth was often used to support a greater number of children. In addition, children themselves were used in preindustrial production, thus producing more wealth for their families. Each succeeding mode of production, therefore, led to an increase in population (which put further pressure on both the environment and on expanding the existing mode of production).
10. With industrialization, the development of modern birth control techniques and changes in structures and superstructures, the relationship between the growth in the mode of production and population has been broken (see Harris 1981, 76–97 for an extended discussion of the demographic transition).
11. Infrastructures of societies, that is, a society's mode of production and its population, put very strong constraints on the range of widespread social institutions, ideas, and ideologies of sociocultural systems.
12. Structural elites provide positive and negative feedback to infrastructural change. The interests of the elite will weigh more heavily than others. This feedback can often be decisive in determining whether infrastructural change is amplified and propagated throughout the social system or whether it is extinguished.
13. Cultural superstructures provide positive and negative feedback for structural and infrastructural changes. Superstructural feedback can be critical, particularly if a society exploits its environment to the point of "absolute" depletion (that is, the costs of raw materials become prohibitive). If a sociocultural system does not have the cultural knowledge base to switch to a new mode of production based on a new resource base, that system will collapse.
14. Sociocultural adaptation and change are based on the alteration of existing structures and behavior patterns. The force of historical experience, therefore, plays a major role in shaping social institutions and thought.
15. Unlike biological evolution, social evolution is a Lamarckian process; that is, successful adaptations are learned. We do not depend on genetic variability and environmental selection for the preservation of successful

adaptation — we rely on culture. This is what makes social evolution so dynamic.

16. Successful adaptations are spread through social contact and military and economic conquest. Although environmental necessity is the key to understanding pristine change — that is, change that occurs without the benefit of having contact with other societies — the rapid adoption of most technologies and social practices occur through cultural diffusion.

In addition to these general characteristics, Lenski, Nolan, and Lenski take social evolution a step further and suggest that selection favors larger, more powerful societies at the expense of smaller, less powerful ones. There has been a dramatic reduction in the number of societies in the world in the last 10,000 years because of this evolutionary process of intersocietal selection. This process can be summarized in one additional point:

17. Societies that have grown in size and technology have also grown in complexity and military power; this has allowed them to prevail in conflicts over territory and resources with societies that have maintained more traditional sociocultural patterns.

Ecological-evolutionary theoretical discussions of structural and superstructural feedback are limited to descriptions and broad statements that "they matter." Although the theory is highly developed in general concepts and theories that stem from infrastructural-environmental relationships, it suffers from a lack of systematic development of general concepts and theoretical principles of structures and superstructures. This can be remedied with the synthesis of some of the concepts and theories of Max Weber.

Sociocultural materialism is a synthesis of ecological-evolutionary theory with the sociology and insights of Weber. Weber characterized the sweep of human history with his typology of human action and his theory of increasing rationalization. Although Weber's is an evolutionary theory, he did not often root his theory of increasing rationalization and the growth of bureaucracy in ecology. Doing so, however, is not a difficult task:

The intensification of the infrastructure (population and production) leads to the growth of secondary organizations at the expense of primary groups — a process known as bureaucratization. Weber (1946) did address the intensification and bureaucracy relationship at least once: "To this extent increasing bureaucratization is a function of the increasing possession of goods used for consumption, and of an increasingly sophisticated technique of fashioning external life — a technique which corresponds to the opportunities provided by such wealth" (p. 212). The greater the intensification of the infrastructure, the more a formal organization is needed to coordinate and control the complex production processes and large numbers of people.

This bureaucratization of structure changes the cultural superstructure of a society, which changes the character of the men and women who make up the society. Weber classified these changes under the rubric of rationalization. According to Weber, observation, experiment, and reason to master the natural and social environment to achieve a desired end guide human behavior. This growth of goal-oriented behavior is at the expense of behavior that is guided by emotions, traditions, or ultimate human values.

The rationalization of the superstructure provides positive feedback for the continuing bureaucratization of structure. Bureaucratization is the increasing application of logic, observation, and reason to problems posed by human organization. The relationship between rationalization and bureaucratization is straight out of Weber; the direction of the relationship is consistent with the ecological-evolutionary concept of feedback (see point 13, earlier).

The rationalization of the superstructure and bureaucratization of structure provide strong positive feedback to the intensification process. The intensification process itself can be interpreted as another particular case of rationalization — the increasing application of observation, logic, and reason and the decline of values, traditions, and emotions — within the infrastructure. Weber's rationalization process can also characterize the changing relationship between production and population growth in industrial societies (see point 10, earlier). Again, the direction of the relationship is consistent with cultural ecology's emphasis on feedback.

The growth of bureaucracy and the increase in power this gives to elites provide strong positive feedback to the intensification of the mode of production. The relationship between bureaucracy and authority is consistent with Weber's definition of the efficiency and power of organizations to attain their goals as well as his conception of the nature of authority. It is also consistent with ecologists' focus on the role of elites in determining stability and change in the sociocultural system (see point 12, earlier).

The more a sociocultural system has rationalized the larger the potential population size and the more technologically powerful that society will be. In accordance with Lenski (see point 17, earlier), such societies will be "much more likely to survive and transmit their cultures and institutional patterns than societies that have preserved traditional social and cultural patterns and minimized innovations" (Lenski, Nolan, & Lenski 1995, 71).

Modes of production limit widespread social structures (that is, family, economic, government) and superstructures (ideas, ideologies, and even entire cultural world views). Structures and superstructural ideas may influence further infrastructural intensification. Up to this point I have written of the general trend of rationalization in the cultural superstructure. Now, I turn to a specific expression of rationalization in industrial superstructures — the technological world view. Rooted in industrial society's relation to its environment, the technological world view represents a constellation of such beliefs as faith in material progress; technology can solve any problems, natural or social; and all can truly benefit from the creation of more material wealth. This faith in the wonders of technology is mainly based on the past success of industrial societies. However, there is a theoretical basis to this faith as well — a basis that lies in the refutation of T. Robert Malthus, whose *Essay on Population* in 1798 was intended to show the futility of economic and social progress.

MALTHUS AND PROGRESS

Industrial societies promote belief in progress — faith in the wonders of technology and organization in ever more efficiently exploiting our environment. Bill Gates neatly summarizes the technological world view — a symbolic image of the relationship of technology, population, and the environment — and takes a swipe at Malthus in the process:

> By and large, technology is a positive force that can help us solve even our most vexing potential problems. Two centuries ago the economist Thomas Malthus warned of the dangers of compounding population increases. Overpopulation remains a potentially ominous problem, given the effect of exponential growth, but recent trends are encouraging: Population growth slows as technology increases affluence and improves education. Environmental problems and resource shortages must be taken seriously too, but I think many doomsayers vastly underestimate the potential of technology to help us overcome these problems. (Gates 1996, 291)

The technologists argue that technology has kept up with population growth in the past and that it will continue to do so in the future. Malthus, they believe, did not take into account the potential of technology to increase the subsistence base. They also claim that Malthus neglected to explore the issue of widespread birth control. Finally, this first of all demographers, they believe, knew nothing of the demographic transition — the relationship of affluence and population growth, and so Malthus has been refuted, proved wrong yet again. "So Malthus was wrong. Over and over again he was wrong. No other prophet has ever been proved wrong so many times" (McKibben 1998, 59). Yet, as McKibben well knows, Malthus has yet to be refuted.

There are several problems with this refutation of Malthus. First, technologists tend to misstate Malthus's position (actually they are not alone in this, many people who are sympathetic to Malthus's argument often misstate his position). Malthus just did not predict that population would grow until the environment could no longer support it. In fact, he stated that if that is all we had to worry about, why worry at all:

> An event at such a distance might fairly be left to providence, but the truth is that if the view of the argument given in this Essay be just, the difficulty, so far from being remote, would be imminent and immediate. At every period during the progress of cultivation, from the present moment to the time when the whole earth was become like a garden, the distress for want of food would be constantly pressing on all mankind, if they were equal. [Of course, Malthus knows mankind does not distribute resources equally.] Though the produce of the earth might be increasing every year, population would be increasing much faster, and the redundancy must necessarily be repressed by the periodical or constant action of misery or vice. (Malthus 1798)

Malthus was not worried about a world population explosion that would outstrip the resource base in some distant future. He was concerned with the consequences of an imbalance between our ability to produce food and our ability to produce children in all past, present, and future societies. Because of this imbalance, the poor would always be among us, inequality is built into the structure of human societies, and the creation of a technological paradise for all was simply not feasible. Malthus summarized his theory:

> I think I may fairly make two postulata. First, That food is necessary to the existence of man. Secondly, That the passion between the sexes is necessary and will remain nearly in its present state. Assuming then my postulata as granted, I say, that the power of population is indefinitely greater than the power in the earth to produce subsistence for man. Population, when unchecked, increases in a geometrical ratio. Subsistence increases only in an arithmetical ratio. A slight acquaintance with numbers will [shew] the immensity of the first power in comparison of the second. By that law of our nature which makes food necessary to the life of man, the effects of these two unequal powers must be kept equal. This implies a strong and constantly operating check on population from the

difficulty of subsistence. This difficulty must fall somewhere and must necessarily be severely felt by a large portion of mankind. (Malthus 1798)

There are two types of checks on population, Malthus wrote; checks that must necessarily operate on a large proportion of mankind. One type, positive checks, includes famine, war, unwholesome occupations, disease, misery, and vice (for example, drug abuse or alcoholism). Malthus labeled these positive checks (oh, what an unfortunate choice of terminology!) because they actively cut down existing population by reducing the human life span. Positive checks operate on the poor and powerless much more than on the well-to-do and elites.

Malthus also considered some preventive checks, including contraception and celibacy. Celibacy, he stated, is not a viable option for human beings — at least for large numbers of people. Contraception, he stated, may act to check population, but there are two problems with it. First, contraception is likely to be used by the most educated and wealthy classes — not by the poor who feel the full brunt of positive checks. Second, the widespread use of contraception would change the moral behavior of men and women and have inevitable effects on family and community life.

The frequent pronouncements that Malthus was wrong because modern technology has been able to stretch the resource base without limit are seriously flawed. There are strong and constantly operating positive checks on human population. These checks operated in the past, they operate now, and will probably continue to operate in the future. That 20 to 30 percent of the world's population live in affluent, industrial societies does not disprove Malthus's contention. There are significant inequalities within industrial societies, many of which lead to higher mortality rates for poorer people. More important, in terms of numbers, there are tremendous inequalities between societies. Third World societies are central to industrial countries because they have raw materials and provide markets for industrial goods. They are also a source of cheap labor. More than 70 percent of the world's population live in Third World countries — and the percentage is growing. In many countries, famine, war, and disease are widespread; life spans are greatly shortened; and birth rates and infant mortality are high. These sorts of positive checks, Malthus predicted, will always be needed. The technologists may counter that food shortages are not caused by the lack of productive capacity because our present technology is capable of feeding every child, woman, and man on earth if food was distributed equally (at least at this point in time). The problem is, of course, that such resources are not distributed equally. Some people get far more than others, which is precisely what Malthus said must happen:

positive checks must operate on a large proportion of mankind — mainly on the poor and the powerless.

The constant positive checks on population — war, famine, and disease — are unacceptable to the civilized mind. The technological fix, then, is to turn to one of the preventive checks — the easy one of contraception. Modern thinkers tend to dismiss Malthus's moral opinion of contraception — Malthus was a minister, and his rigid morality has already given way in advanced industrial societies. Birth control and its effects on moral behavior do not seem so shocking to our ear, especially when compared with the positive checks. Technological developments in birth control techniques provide us with excellent individual control over contraception and, most importantly, we have found the keys to motivating humans to use this contraception on a widespread basis.

The technological world view holds that by stimulating economic development and education we can encourage families to voluntarily limit the number of children, through contraception, because it is in their interests to do so. (This, coincidentally, is consistent with Malthus's view that only the economically well off and educated would use birth control on a widespread basis.) People will voluntarily limit the number of their children because children in advanced industrial societies are no longer economic assets; in fact, they become significant economic liabilities. So it is through economic development that we can achieve the voluntary actions of families to limit their family size. Society as a whole would thereby achieve the "demographic transition" — a stabilization of population. Furthermore, it is through technology that we can sustain huge population levels.

However, there is an additional problem (aside from Malthus's concern with morals) with the potential of voluntary birth control to serve as an effective preventive check on population. Preventive checks, voluntary limits on population growth, can be achieved through the economic development of poor countries. The problem lies with the implausibility of stimulating significant economic growth among the 70 to 80 percent of the world's population who live in Third World economies so that they can achieve this demographic transition. This is particularly true when population growth rates are higher than economic growth rates. Each year many societies experience a decrease in their standard of living and are further away from turning the corner in the demographic transition. Also, the national debt is already very high in many Third World countries; many are having trouble paying interest on existing debt for previous development schemes; they are not good candidates for more loans to stimulate development.

Let us suppose that a combination of economic development, education, and totalitarian decree stabilizes the population on earth — world population is currently expected to stabilize in the next century at 10 to 11 billion (almost double our present population). The technological solution to maintaining this high population is through the use of more technology and organization to more efficiently exploit our environments. This will require a tremendous technological infrastructure, but the environmental problems associated with population growth — pollution and depletion of resources — are even more strongly related to economic growth than to population. Althougheconomic development may be able to keep population down, it does so by stimulating the desire for goods and services, a solution that is worse than the population expansion itself.

Being consistent with Malthus, Harris (1977, 282–283) points out that in the contest of man versus nature there can be no final victory. The race is never over; any technological advantage can be only temporary. Each year our technology is called upon to wrest more resources from a depleting environment. In order to sustain our lifestyles, Americans consume almost one-third of the world's annual production of energy — 70 times as much energy as is used by a Bangladeshi; 20 times as much as a Costa Rican (McKibben 1998). Few economists envision future Third World societies consuming energy and resources at rates as high as America does. The combination of high population and a moderate industrial infrastructure to provide necessary goods and services could be an ecological disaster. Can we have the industrial good life for the 10 billion people projected for 2050? Can the earth tolerate the greenhouse gases that such development would produce? Can earth tolerate even more ozone destruction? Is there enough water for agriculture? Is there enough fuel for our cars, planes, and homes? Can the earth sustain such development for a year? Can earth sustain such development for hundreds of years? To these questions and others the proponents of the technological world view answer: "I think many doomsayers vastly underestimate the potential of technology to help us overcome these problems" (Gates 1996, 291).

Positive checks on population — wars, genocide, famine, and disease — decrease human longevity. Whether economic development will be attainable, sufficient, and sustainable enough to negate the positive checks on the vast numbers of humans cannot be known. We do know, however, that a significant proportion of children, women, and men have been denied opportunities to share in the wealth of nations — and that positive Malthusian checks have been very active throughout human history in decimating this population. Perhaps the technologists are right — that technological solutions can create the industrial good-life for billions;

perhaps they vastly overestimate the potential of technology and underestimate the power of nature.

CONCLUSION

In a book that purports to be about industrial systems it may seem strange to devote an entire chapter to sociocultural evolution and an extended discussion of the ideas of Thomas Malthus. There are reasons for its inclusion: "It all fits together" (one of my favorite lines that drives my students up a wall). This chapter was designed to demonstrate the power of sociocultural materialism — the centrality of production and population in the social system and the importance of feedback from structures and superstructures. Another goal of writing this brief sketch of the social evolutionary process and the rise of the technological world view is that it sets the historical stage for a discussion of industrialism itself. Sociocultural evolution is not simply one of theoretical or historical interest; today's basic system organization is the same. Advanced industrial societies are still subject to environmental constraints, which are passed on through the infrastructure to social structures and cultures — forces that have, in turn, guided change from the beginning and are still at work. In the next chapter we will examine the role and power of elites in industrial sociocultural systems, specifically, the role of elites in promoting continued industrial intensification.

3

Structures of Authority

Paranoia runs deep. Many people see conspiracies that control society (just look at the popular television show, X-Files, in which "cancer man" has participated in everything from the Kennedy assassinations to making sure the Buffalo Bills never win a Super Bowl). Conspiracy theories range from international bankers to the Trilateral Commission, from the Central Intelligence Agency to a business elite that cynically pull the strings of governments. Some see energy companies suppressing inventions of solar power or engines that run on water. Many profess to see the machinations of a military-industrial complex, which drums up fear and takes untold wealth from the nation. People see conspiracies because they lack power and control over their own lives. They see conspiracies because certain groups do consistently benefit from events. The idea of conspiracy is attractive because it points to an easy mechanism of power: secret meetings for coordination and the cynical manipulation of people, governments, and markets. Although they are popular and attractive, the bulk of these theories are misleading. This chapter is an attempt to disabuse the reader of notions of conspiracy. It is an introduction to the concepts and practices of organizational power, which make theories of national or global conspiracy unnecessary.

Max Weber noted that by its very nature a bureaucracy generates an enormous degree of unregulated and often unperceived social power. Because of bureaucracies' superiority over other forms of organization, they have proliferated and now dominate modern societies. Those who control these organizations, Weber warned, control the quality of our life, and they are largely self-appointed leaders. Bureaucracy tends to result in oligarchy, or rule by the few officials at the top of the organization. In a society dominated by large formal organizations, social, political, and economic power will become concentrated in the hands of the few who hold high positions in the most influential of these organizations (Weber 1921, 196–244).

Robert Michels, a sociologist and friend of Max Weber, came to the conclusion that the problem lay in the nature of organizations. He formulated the "Iron Law of Oligarchy," which states: "Who says organization, says oligarchy" (Michels 1915, 15). Any large organization, Michels pointed out, is faced with administrative problems that can be solved only by creating a bureaucracy. A bureaucracy, in turn, is hierarchically organized to efficiently attain goals. The effective functioning of an organization, therefore, requires the concentration of much power in the hands of a few people. In effect, this concentration of power separates most individuals from control over the decisions that affect their lives. "In theory the leader is merely an employee bound by the instruction he receives. He has to carry out the orders of the mass, of which he is no more than the executive organ. But in actual fact, as the organization increases in size, this control becomes purely fictitious" (Michels 1915, 71). This is easy to see if one is a member of an organization, because key decision-making authority flows to administrative officers at the top. People who work within a bureaucracy (and many modern people do) directly experience the loss of work autonomy and freedom.

Michels also pointed out that certain characteristics of both leaders and members of organizations reinforce the organizational characteristics that promote an oligarchy. People achieve leadership positions precisely because they have unusual political skills; they are adept at getting their way and persuading others of the correctness of their views. Once they hold high office, their power and prestige are further increased. Leaders have access and control over information and facilities that are not available to the rank-and-file and they control the information that flows down the channels of communication. Leaders are also strongly motivated to persuade the organization of the rightness of their views; and they use all of their skills, power, and authority to do so. By design, rank-and-file members are less informed than their "superiors." Holding an office within the organization enhances the personal qualities of the leaders. From birth, we are taught to obey those who are in positions of authority. Therefore, the rank-and-file tend to look to leaders for policy directives and are generally prepared to allow leaders to exercise their judgment on most matters.

Leaders also have control over very powerful negative and positive sanctions to promote the behavior they desire. They have the power to grant or deny raises, assign workloads, fire, demote, and, that most gratifying of all sanctions, the power to promote. Most important, they tend to promote junior officials who share their opinions, with the result that the oligarchy becomes self-perpetuating. Therefore, the very nature of large-scale organization makes oligarchy within bureaucracies inevitable (Michels 1915).

The "iron law of oligarchy" extends beyond the internal workings of organizations. A bureaucracy is a social technology for coordinating and controlling complex tasks. As bureaucracies proliferate and grow within a society, more and more social power is placed within their control. Modern industrial societies are increasingly dominated by large, complex organizations. All societies with any degree of complexity are, therefore, elitist. Elitism is not the result of conspiracies, it is an integral part of any complex organization. Although all societies have elites, the power of elites varies across societies and through time. Sources of variance in the power of elites include the size and scope of the bureaucratic structures they lead: The larger the bureaucratic organization, the more wealth it controls and the greater the social power it is able to generate. The more centralized a bureaucracy becomes, the more this power is placed into fewer hands. Bureaucracies, and therefore the elite who control them, have become powerful and centralized in the modern industrial world, but it is through organization that individuals lose control of the decision-making process.

SOCIETAL OLIGARCHY

It is easy to see oligarchy within formal organizations, but Weber's views on the inevitability of oligarchy within whole societies are a little subtler. In his view, bureaucracies are necessary to provide the coordination and control that are so desperately needed by our complex production processes and huge populations. "The decisive reason for the advance of bureaucratic organization has always been its purely technical superiority over any other form of organization. The fully developed bureaucratic mechanism compares with other organizations exactly as does the machine with the non-mechanical modes of production" (Weber 1946, 214). Whereas modern societies are dependent on formal organization, a bureaucracy tends to undermine both human freedom and democracy. As bureaucracy grows it comes to dominate the social structure of modern society — bureaucratic goals, procedures, and hierarchy play an increasing role in social life.

The enlargement and centralization of government power in industrialized nations has been remarkable in the twentieth century. "At the beginning of this century government spending in today's industrial countries accounted for less than one-tenth of national income. Last year, in the same countries, the government's share of output was roughly half" (*The Economist* 1997a, S7). This growth has been going on decade after decade, in good economic times and bad. Even in societies that have tried to drastically control government spending — Margaret Thatcher's Conservative Government of Britain for example — the impact on the government's share of total income has been negligible (*The Economist* 1997a).

In the United States the federal, state, and local governments' shares of national income is somewhat less than in most other industrialized nations; even here, in this bastion of laissez-faire capitalism, government spending has increased from about 2 percent of the economy in 1913, to approximately 33 percent of the gross domestic product today (*The Economist* 1997a). This growth is even more remarkable when we consider that the total economic "pie" has grown tremendously as well. Today's economy is about 20 times larger than it was in 1900, but total government expenditures are 65 times larger. More recent growth in American government spending is also remarkable — rising about 20 percent since 1960 (though this is modest when compared with the 60 percent average rise internationally) (*The Economist* 1997a).

Corporate growth and concentration have also been intensifying. Huge corporations have long dominated industrial economies. Although centralization was well advanced in the earlier part of the twentieth century, the pace quickened after World War II. As a result the proportion of all industrial assets controlled by the largest 100 corporations has grown from 39.8 percent in 1950 to 58.3 percent in 1983 (Dye 1986, 16), and the pace quickens. The decade of the 1980s was the era of "merger mania." The wave of mergers in the 1990s makes the 1980s look like small change. According to Miller, "The global M&A [mergers & acquisitions] market broke all records last year at $1 trillion and at its current pace will hit $1.3 trillion this year. (The biggest year of the '80s was 1989: $600 billion.)" (Miller 1997, 279). Government growth and corporate growth both set the stage for societal oligarchy.

Democratic theory has it that government is ultimately responsible to the people, but this accountability is largely illusory. In reality it often happens that the electorate does not even know what its governments are doing. Government departments have grown so numerous and complex that they cannot be supervised effectively. Huge corporations, economic bureaucracies that have tremendous effects on our lives, over which we have little control, further compound the problem. Our control over corporations is hardly even fictional any longer. Not only do these economic bureaucracies affect us directly, they also affect our governments — organizations that are supposedly designed to regulate them.

Coincidental with the centralization of power is its enlargement in the modern world. The key decision makers have instruments to influence the masses, such as television, advertising, and public relations firms, and techniques of propaganda that are unsurpassed in the history of humankind. Finally, the tremendous advances in transportation and communication have made it much more likely that organizations can coordinate and project this power around the globe in an efficient manner. These developments place more power in the hands of elites at the top of organizations, and they also make the decisions of elites more consequential. In short, the institutional structures of authority (and the people at the top of them) have a significant effect on public policy. To discuss society and social change without referring to the power and interests of the elite is to engage in empty academic exercise.

THE POWER ELITE

Although theories of elite domination have been around for centuries, it was C. Wright Mills who, in 1956, provided the framework for current elite theories in his book *The Power Elite*. According to Mills, the power elite are the key people in the three major institutions of modern society: central government, military, and corporations. These institutions have become larger, more powerful, and more centralized in their decision making. Together, the leaders of these institutions are a unified elite that, while not omnipotent, is formidable. "They occupy the strategic command posts of the social structure, in which are now centered the effective means of power and wealth and the celebrity which they enjoy" (Mills 1956, 4). The elites are those few people who have formal authority over our lives. Through their institutional positions, the power elite control the key bureaucracies in industrial societies. Thus, power is transformed into authority, an attribute of social organizations, not of individuals.

By asserting that there is a power elite in American society, Mills was not asserting that there is a self-conscious ruling class, which is cynically manipulating the masses. It is not a conspiracy of evil men, he argued, but a social structure that enlarged and centralized the decision-making process and power and then placed this power in the hands of men of similar social background and outlook.

In Mills's view, major national power now resides almost exclusively in the economic, political, and military domains. All other institutions have diminished in scope and power and been made subordinate to the big three. "Families and churches and schools adapt to modern life; governments and armies and corporations shape it; and, as they do so, they turn these lesser institutions into means for their ends. . . . And the symbols of these lesser institutions are used to legitimate the power and decisions of the big three" (Mills 1956, 6). Schools have become appendages of corporations and government, sorting and training young people for their corporate careers, and in so doing inculcating patriotism, respect for authority, and the glories of capitalism. Families have lost their political and productive functions; they now serve largely as consumption units and as suppliers of workers and soldiers to the bureaucratic-industrial state. Families are still major socialization agents of the young, but they now share this function with schools and the mass media. Through the socialization process, each of us has come to accept the system as it is. A general consensus on what is right and natural is forged. The interests of the elites are legitimized. "The interests of an economically dominant class never stand naked. They are enshrouded in the flag, fortified by the law, protected by the police, nurtured by the media, taught by the schools, and blessed by the church" (Parenti 1978, 84). All of these trends serve to legitimize and strengthen the power and authority of the big three.

It is their similar social backgrounds that provide one of the major sources of unity among the elite. The majority of the elite, Mills asserted, come from the upper third of the income and occupational pyramids. They are closely linked through intermarriages, private preparatory schools, Ivy League universities, and exclusive gentleman's clubs. Non–upper-class members of the elite consist of hired corporate managers, experts, and corporate lawyers—men who are competent technocrats, who have risen through the ranks, and are subsequently sponsored by the elite and the organizations they control.

Of the three sectors of institutional power, Mills implied that the corporate elite is perhaps the most powerful, but he asserted that the power elite cannot be understood as a mere reflection of economic elites; rather, it is the alliance (albeit sometimes uneasy) of economic, political, and military power.

Mills saw two other levels in American society below the power elite. At the bottom are the great masses of people—largely unorganized, ill-informed, and virtually powerless. Controlled and manipulated from above, they are economically and politically exploited. Between the masses and the elite are the middle levels of power. Composed of local opinion leaders and special interest groups, they neither represent the masses nor have any real effect on the elite. Mills saw the American Congress as a reflection of this middle-level power. Although Congress decides some minor issues, the power elite ensures that no serious challenge to its authority and control is tolerated in the political arena.

More recent writings in the elitist tradition tend to credit Congress with more power than Mills's view. The power that Congress has to investigate the decisions of the executive branch is still considerable. Political action committees distribute money to legislators who support their interests. People of wealth often back promising politicians early in their careers by sponsoring those who are sympathetic to their views. The political parties, then, are constrained to choose candidates whose views are congruent with those of the economic elites. Although most contemporary elite theorists assert that corporations are among the most active and successful of all lobbyists, few claim that Congress is completely dominated by business elites. Most theorists also tend to believe that military personnel do not participate in the power elite (at least in Western nations). Theorists point out that high-ranking military officers come from different classes and regions than do the elites of government and business. Furthermore, whereas some military leaders do attain important corporate and governmental posts, it is not common (it may have been more common in Mills's day; this may have been the result of America's experience with World War II and the Cold War). Also, by 1958 Mills seemed much more concerned with the rise of militarism among elites than with the hypothesis that many elites were military men. Most elite theorists now see the military as dominated by the executive branch of government. Contemporary elite theorists have provided considerable evidence and refinement of Mills's basic hypothesis, but they have also uncovered some evidence that calls into question the extent of explicit coordination among the elite.

WHO IS RUNNING AMERICA?

Thomas Dye has written a series of books (one every four years or so) that attempt to empirically gauge the concentration of power in American society. In 1986 Dye divided American society into 12 dominant sectors: industrial corporations; utilities, transportation, and communications; banking; insurance; investments; mass media; law; education; foundations; civic and cultural organizations; government; and the military. In each of these fields, Dye attempted to empirically identify the number of organizations that dominate each sector. For example, in 1983, of the 200,000 or so industrial corporations in the United States with total assets of about $1.6 trillion, the largest 100 corporations controlled 58.2 percent ($939 billion) of the assets. In the financial world, the concentration is even greater. Of the 14,763 banks that served America in 1983, the largest 50 controlled 64 percent of all banking assets. The top ten insurance companies, out of a field of 2,048, controlled 55 percent of all insurance assets (Dye 1986, 16–23).

In all, Dye identified about 4,300 positions at the top of these organizations that dominate the corporate sector of American life (utilities; heavy industry; and communications, transportation, banking, insurance, and investment corporations). These people are the presidents, chief officers, and members of the boards of directors of America's largest corporations. In addition, Dye included 2,700 leaders in the public interest sectors (that is, mass media; education; foundations; and law, civic, and cultural organizations) and about 300 in national government and the military. There are so few positions because economic, social, and political power in America is highly concentrated in just a few organizations that concentrate a great amount of power in just a few people at the top.

Dye also examined evidence of the alleged increasingly explicit coördination within and among corporate and government institutions. Many elite theorists claim that, since World War II, business and government have become increasingly intertwined. The executive branch of government has grown with new regulatory agencies, commissions, and advisory councils that patrol, protect, and coordinate the complex national economy — agencies and commissions that are usually staffed by corporate men. Corporate and government planning have replaced the market place in many sectors of the American economy. Elite organizations such as the Council on Foreign Relations, the Business Roundtable, and the Committee for Economic Development also help coordinate national policies. Elitists claim that this coordination between the elites is not total, but it is an important source of unity for elite interests.

Dye uncovered some evidence of explicit coordination within the corporate sector. Of the 7,314 top institutional positions in the 12 sectors of society, he identified only 5,778 individuals who occupied these positions. In other words, some elites hold more than one position of leadership in American society. Because some individuals hold three or more positions, approximately 30 percent of all elite positions identified by Dye are interlocked with other elite positions. (This percentage undoubtedly would have been far higher if Dye had included the elites who hold multiple corporate and civic posts but who do not hold one of the 7,314 positions in the dominant organizations as defined by Dye.) Dye noted that these interlockers hold multiple directorships of large corporate and financial institutions, foundations, universities, and civic associations. Dye believed that their multiple positions encourage them to take a broad view of corporate problems. It is this inner group that coordinates the activities of a variety of bureaucratic organizations. "They move from the industrial point of interest and outlook to the interest and outlook of all big corporate property as a whole" (Mills 1956, 121).

Dye found significant consensus among his identified elites over basic values and the future directions of American society, but he does not believe this consensus is the product of explicit coordination through interlocking positions, recruitment, common class, or more informal socializing among the elite. Although there is much evidence of coordination within the corporate and public-interest sector elites (and between these two groups), government and military leaders do not fit this pattern.

For example, Dye did not find much evidence of an interlocking overlap between government and military leaders and the other sectors of society (which is not too surprising because most laws forbid serving on corporate boards while holding a government or military office). Dye did find that there was a record of interlocking between government leaders and those in other sectors over the course of a government official's entire career, but only one quarter of Dye's identified top government leaders ever held top positions in the corporate world; most government leaders gained their experience in law or other professions (Dye 1986, 184).

Dye also found minimal evidence that government elites are recruited from the same stratum as corporate elites. Whereas corporate leaders have a "slight" tendency to come from the upper class and have attended prep schools and Ivy League colleges, government leaders make it to the top through careers in law and other professional fields, as well as through the ranks of government itself.

Dye found minimal evidence of the importance of private-club memberships for government and military elites. Whereas nearly two-thirds of the corporate elite held private club memberships (one-third held five or more such memberships) only 23.7 percent of government leaders were members of private clubs (Dye 1986, 216). The proportion of military leaders who belonged to private clubs was significantly less.

Dye (1983; 1986) provided significant empirical evidence for Mills's assertion that power is growing and centralizing in huge bureaucracies with a few command posts at the top. Evidence of explicit coordination between corporate and government elites, however, is mixed. I believe Dye had a tendency to minimize the extent of explicit coordination between government and corporate elites. Admittedly, the evidence of explicit coordination between government and corporate elites is not overwhelming, although Dye did report consensus on the goals of the elite. How, then, do government and corporate elites achieve their consensus over basic policies and the future directions of American society?

THE CORPORATE STATE

Mills argued that coordination between government and corporations did not always depend on back-room meetings, private clubs, interlocking, or being from the same social class. (Mills, too, recognized that many elites are recruited from classes other than the rich.) Mills saw that a good part of the coordination came from a growing structural integration of the dominant institutions:

> As each of these domains becomes enlarged and centralized, the consequences of its activities become greater, and its traffic with the others increases. The decisions of a handful of corporations bear upon military and political as well as upon economic developments around the world. The decisions of the military establishment rest upon and grievously affect political life as well as the very level of economic activity. The decisions made within the political domain determine economic activities and military programs. There is no longer, on the one hand, an economy, and, on the other hand, a political order containing a military establishment unimportant to politics and to money-making. There is a political economy linked, in a thousand ways, with military institutions and decisions. . . . There is an ever-increasing interlocking of economic, military, and political structures. If there is government intervention in the corporate economy, so is there corporate intervention in the governmental process. In the structural

> sense, this triangle of power is the source of the interlocking directorate that is most important for the historical structure of the present. (Mills 1956, 7–8)

The search for explicit coordination among elites mirrors the popular search for conspiracies. Such an expectation of conspiracy serves to understate the structured bias of government and corporate leaders toward one another's interests.

According to Michael Harrington, the very institutions of government — even when they are not under the direct influence of elites who represent their class interests — will follow corporate priorities. Harrington emphasized that the modern state is not a mere tool of corporations; it is not a conscious, conspiratorial phenomenon; the elites do not have an omniscient and objective sense of their interests; nor are they all-powerful in achieving their goals. Rather, because the dominant economic institutions in modern society are private corporations, the government must follow corporate priorities. "The welfare-state government is not itself the initiator of most production within the economy. The corporations do that. However, that same government is increasingly charged with arranging the preconditions for profitable production. Its funds, its power, its political survival, depend on private sector performance. So do the jobs of most workers. The state's interest in perpetuating its own rule is thus, in economic fact, identified with the health of the capitalist economy" (Harrington 1976, 307).

Harrington gave numerous examples of how the modern state formulates social policies that benefit corporate America, and, in the process, often worsen (or create) problems that the government then deplores. American agriculture, Harrington pointed out, is dominated by gigantic agribusinesses. In 1971, for example, nearly 80 percent of all agricultural income was earned by only about 20 percent of the largest farms. These farms receive tens of billions of dollars in federal subsidies, which allow corporate farms to replace independent farmers at enormous taxpayer expense. It makes good political sense to fashion agricultural policy so that it benefits organizations that have economic and political power. Even without direct contact with agribusiness elites, the state will follow corporate priorities when farm policies are established. Harrington also documented corporate bias in government policies on highways, energy use, urban affairs, and housing.

According to Harrington, the state promotes the corporate economy through four actions. First, the state allows the formation of multinational corporate oligopolies and cartels to promote managerial planning and eliminate the vagaries of the market. Second, the government subsidizes

Cartel- a combination of businesses to control production and avoid competition technological innovation to create new needs and markets. Third, government subsidizes many private industries through massive defense spending. Fourth, the state engages in direct intervention in the economy to offset inflation and recession and depression cycles.

Even in capitalist societies, Harrington was quick to point out, elites have some limits on their power. The history and constitutional structure of a given society provide some limits on the power of elites. In a society dominated by large corporations, federal government policies cannot run counter to the interest of the corporate sector "unless they have the support of a determined mass movement willing to fight for structural change" (Harrington 1976, 223). In the last 30 years, many interest groups aside from big business have grown in size and power. Civil rights organizations, environmental groups, feminist groups, the Christian right, and antinuclear groups have all developed specific agendas. The modern state, according to Harrington, can be seen as a result of some compromise between these interest groups and the corporate elite. Sometimes the goals of the interest groups are achieved because they do not directly conflict with those of the corporate structure. Other goals are attained because they ameliorate some of the worst abuses of corporate capitalism and are reluctantly conceded to by elites to head off popular discontent. Finally, some of the goals of the interest groups directly conflict. Such issues as environmental protection and consumer- and worker-safety cost corporate America dearly. The elites resist these types of structural reforms by using all available resources (including the use and abuse of science and social science). Both sides use propaganda and half-truths to advance their positions. More often than not, because the structure is systematically biased to favor elite interests, the elites prevail. At times, however, when opposition is tightly organized and the masses are sufficiently aroused, corporate elites must grant some reforms.

Given that national governments increasingly are being held accountable for the health of their economies, the modern state cannot consistently act counter to the fundamental interests of private corporations. What are the interests of corporate America? What are the interests of the elite? Before turning to these questions, it is first necessary to explore one other characteristic of bureaucracy that Weber noted, the irrationality factor.

THE IRRATIONALITY FACTOR

Because it is clear that modern societies are dominated by bureaucracy, it is crucial to understand why this enormous power is often used for ends that are counter to the interests and needs of people. Weber maintained that even though a bureaucracy is highly rational in the formal sense of technical efficiency, it does not follow that the moral acceptability of a bureaucracy's goals or the means used to achieve them is also rational. Nor does an exclusive focus on the goals of an organization necessarily coincide with the broader goals of society as a whole. It often happens that the single-minded pursuit of practical goals can actually undermine the foundations of the social order. What is good for a bureaucracy is not always good for society as a whole — and, often, in the long term, is not good for a bureaucracy either.

Human Radiation Experiments

On January 15, 1994, President Clinton appointed the Advisory Committee on Human Radiation Experiments to investigate reports of possibly unethical human experiments funded by the government from 1944 to 1974. The findings of the committee were first issued in a 937-page report (1995) and were posted on the World Wide Web to promote public access (Department of Energy, 1998). Although many of the experiments conducted were within accepted scientific practice, some were clearly beyond these bounds. The committee found that the Office of Human Radiation Experiments put radioactive iron in the food at a boy's school; radiated the genitals of prisoners; injected plutonium into 18 individuals; and forced soldiers to watch a nuclear explosion (half with eye protection, half without). Also revealed was the government-sponsored study of uranium miners who were subject to radon exposures well in excess of known hazardous levels. "The government failed to reduce the hazard by ventilating the mines, and it failed to adequately warn the miners" (Department of Energy 1998). Several hundred miners subsequently died of lung cancer.

The advisory committee was "troubled" by the selection methods used in many of the experiments. It seemed that relatively powerless and easily exploited groups — hospitalized patients, children, and African Americans — were predominantly selected (Department of Energy 1998). One physician-researcher reported that because many of the subjects were receiving treatment at the research facility free of charge, they were expected to participate. The committee was also concerned that many of the medical experiments, despite existing guidelines of the day, failed to obtain a subject's informed consent.

The committee made numerous recommendations on future ethical conduct of research. Two of the principles, however, recur repeatedly as we consider the ethics of past experiments. These are: “One ought not to treat people as mere means to the ends of others,” and “one ought not to inflict harm or risk of harm” (Department of Energy 1998). People were treated as a means to an end in the government’s goal of promoting national security (most of these unethical experiments were conducted at the height of the Cold War) and the medical research goal of learning more about the physiological reaction to radiation.

General Motors — An Insider’s Example:

In a chapter titled “How Moral Men Make Immoral Decisions,” John De Lorean, a former General Motors executive (and famous for many things), mused over business morality:

> It seemed to me, and still does, that the system of American business often produces wrong, immoral and irresponsible decisions, even though the personal morality of the people running the business is often above reproach. The system has a different morality as a group than the people do as individuals, which permits it to willfully produce ineffective or dangerous products, deal dictatorially and often unfairly with suppliers, pay bribes for business, abrogate the rights of employees by demanding blind loyalty to management or tamper with the democratic process of government through illegal political contributions. (J. Wright 1979, 61–62)

De Lorean speculated that this immorality is connected to the impersonal character of business organization. Morality, he believed, has to do with people: “If an action is viewed primarily from the perspective of its effect on people, it is put into the moral realm” (J. Wright 1979, 62). Never in management circles, De Lorean reported, was any substantial concern raised about the effect of the business practices of General Motors on the environment, consumers, the economy, or American society as a whole.

One of the most well-documented cases of the irrationality factor in business was design problems with the Chevrolet Corvair (the Watergate break-in, the Internal Revenue Service, the Post Office, elections in the 1990s, and the Department of Defense provide plenty of government examples). The Corvair was introduced to the American market in 1960, after several compromises of the original design were made for financial reasons. Before production began, management decided to decrease the tire diameter and delete a $15 stabilizing bar from the suspension system (R. Wright 1996). As a result, a couple of the prototypes rolled over on the test tracks and it quickly became apparent that General Motors had a problem (J. Wright 1979; R. Wright 1996). The engineers were raising serious questions about the safety of the design, but General Motors decided to forge ahead. J. Patrick Wright quoted De Lorean: "The results were disastrous. I don't think any one car before or since produced as gruesome a record on the highway as the Corvair. It was designed and promoted to appeal to the spirit and flair of young people. It was sold in part as a sports car. Young Corvair owners, therefore, were trying to bend their car around curves at high speeds and were killing themselves in alarming numbers" (J. Wright 1979, 66). The denial and cover-up led the corporation to ignore the evidence, even as the number of lawsuits mounted — even as the sons and daughters of executives of the corporation were seriously injured or killed (J. Wright 1979). When Ralph Nader published *Unsafe at Any Speed*, which detailed the Corvair's problems, the response by General Motors was an attempt to cover up its knowledge of the car's problems. Internal documents were destroyed, and executives and engineers alike were pressured to be team players (J. Wright 1979). General Motors assigned a private detective to follow Nader to gather information to attack him personally, rather than debate Nader's facts and assertions (Halberstam 1986; J. Wright 1979; R. Wright 1996). De Lorean summarized the irrational character of the bureaucracy's decision-making process: "There wasn't a man in top GM management who had anything to do with the Corvair who would purposely build a car that he knew would hurt or kill people. But, as part of a management team pushing for increased sales and profits, each gave his individual approval in a group to decisions which produced the car in the face of the serious doubts that were raised about its safety, and then later sought to squelch information which might prove the car's deficiencies" (J. Wright 1979, 65–68). The result was that many immoral decisions were made despite the existence of many moral men within the organization.

An Extreme Case

An extreme case of rationalization was the extermination camps of Nazi Germany. The goal was to kill as many people as possible in the most efficient manner, and the result was the ultimate dehumanization: the murder of millions of men, women and children. The men and women who ran the extermination camps were, in large part, ordinary human beings. They were not particularly evil people; most went to church on Sundays; most had children and loved animals and life.

William Shirer (1966) commented on business firms that collaborated in building and running the camps. Apparently, there was competition among German businessmen for building the crematoria and body disposal machinery and supplying the lethal gas. Shirer offered a 1943 fragment of a letter from I. A. Topf and Sons of Erfurt, manufacturers of heating equipment that built the crematoria at Auschwitz:

> To: The Central Construction Office of the S.S. and Police, Auschwitz
> Subject: Crematoria 2 and 3 for the camp.
>
> We acknowledge receipt of your order for five triple furnaces, including two electric elevators for raising corpses and one emergency elevator. A practical installation for stoking coal was also ordered and one for transporting ashes. (Shirer 1966, 971)

The "lethal blue crystals" of Zyklon-B, which were used in the gas chambers, were supplied by two German firms that had acquired the patent from I. G. Farben (Shirer 1966). Their product could do the most effective job for the least possible cost, so they got the contract. Shirer summarized the organization of evil:

> Before the postwar trials in Germany it had been generally believed that the mass killings were exclusively the work of a relatively few fanatical S.S. leaders. But the records of the courts leave no doubt of the complicity of a number of German businessmen, not only the Krupps and the directors of I.G. Farben chemical trust but smaller entrepreneurs who outwardly must have seemed to be the most prosaic and decent of men, pillars — like good businessmen everywhere — of their communities. (Shirer 1966, 972–973)

In sum, the extermination camps and their suppliers were models of bureaucratic efficiency, which used the most efficient means available at the time to accomplish the goals of the Nazi government.

That individual officials have specialized and limited responsibility and authority within an organization means that they are unlikely to raise basic questions about the moral implications of the overall operation of the organization. Under the rule of specialization, society becomes more and more intricate and interdependent, but with a less common purpose. The community disintegrates because it loses its common bond. The emphasis in bureaucracies is on getting the job done in the most efficient manner possible. Consideration of the effect that organizational behavior might have on society as a whole, on the environment, or on consumers simply does not enter into the calculation. The problem is further compounded by the decline of many traditional institutions, such as the family, community, and religion, which served to bind preindustrial man to the interests of the group. Rationalization causes traditional and religious moral authority to weaken (secularization) so that the values of efficiency and calculability predominate. In an advanced industrial-bureaucratic society, everything, including human beings, becomes a component of the expanding machine.

The result is a paradox — bureaucracies, the epitome of rationalization, acting in irrational ways. C. Wright Mills, who was greatly influenced by Max Weber, wrote of the contradiction between bureaucratic rationality and human reason in social affairs: "A high level of bureaucratic rationality and of technology does not mean a high level of either individual or social intelligence. From the first you cannot infer the second. For social, technological, or bureaucratic rationality is not merely a grand summation of the individual will and capacity to reason. The very chance to acquire that will and that capacity seems in fact often to be decreased by it" (Mills 1959, 168–169). Thus, we have political bureaucracies that are set up to protect our civil liberties but that violate them with impunity; agricultural bureaucracies (and educational, government, and business bureaucracies) that are set up to help the farmer but that end up putting millions of them out of business; service bureaucracies that are designed to care for and protect the elderly but that routinely deny service and actually engage in abuse. The irrationality of bureaucratic institutions is a major factor in understanding contemporary society.

ELITE INTEREST

Thomas Dye is a reluctant elite theorist. Although he admits that his analysis provides strong evidence of a tremendous concentration of power, he tends to minimize the extent of coordination between corporate and government elites. He also points out that many corporate goals conflict (the interests of big oil sometimes conflict with those of automobile manufacturers, for example), and that there are few areas where elite goals are unified. What corporate and government elites do agree on, Dye asserted, are really goals that could be considered "America's goals." Dye stated these goals as follows:

> All have interest in a strong and growing economy, domestic tranquility, and constantly expanding military power. The state is strongly concerned with the stability of the economy. And with its expansion or growth. And with education. And with technical and scientific advance. And, most notably, with the national

defense. These are the national goals; they are sufficiently trite so that one has a reassuring sense of the obvious in articulating them. All have their counterpart in the needs and goals of the techno-structure. It requires stability in demand for its planning. Growth brings promotion and prestige. It requires trained manpower. It needs government underwriting of research and development. Military and other technical procurement support its most developed form of planning. At each point the government has goals with which the techno-structure can identify itself. (Dye 1983, 58–59)

In other words, the structural interests of governmental and corporate elites lie in the continued promotion of economic growth.

It should be noted that growth is not an inherent part of the industrial mode of production. The industrial mode of production consists of rational technologies and social practices that regulate the flow of energy from the environment. The men who control the dominant institutions in our society, both government and corporate, are inextricably committed to economic growth (a commitment they share with governments throughout the world). Through the institutions that dominate the organizational structures of societies, people all over the world have become convinced that unrestrained economic growth is both necessary and desirable. Economic growth is promoted as our only hope of feeding and housing a growing world population, as well as the only hope of improving our own standard of living (indeed, our standard of living has come to be defined in strictly economic terms). Corporate and governmental elites grow more powerful within this consensus on the desirability of economic growth.

Part of the commitment to economic growth stems from the nature of capitalism itself. The objective of capitalism is to maximize the rate of profit as quickly and efficiently as possible. Marvin Harris (1977) explained how companies can most efficiently maximize profits: "A company can increase its rate of profit if it gains technological advantage over its competitors and lowers its unit costs. Technological innovation, therefore, soon becomes the key to the accumulation of capital and business success. Science, in turn, provides the key to technological innovation. Hence, capitalism, science, and scientific technologies form a mutually reinforcing complex" (Harris 1977, 262). To date, industrial socialist societies (both democratic and state socialist) have made the same commitment to expand industrialism.

The goals and drives of the capitalist class are therefore achieved through a growing economy. We measure the health of our economy (as well as the health of the individual corporations that make up the economy) in growth. Increases in gross domestic product, productivity, and profitability are almost universally considered the national priority (even in the nonprofit sector, the health of an institution is increasingly monitored by measures of growth). Not only does this economic growth serve to further enrich the elites, it also serves to protect their acquired wealth from the threat of redistribution.

The demands of the lower classes for increases in income have traditionally been met by increasing economic output. Economic growth is seen as a way of painlessly addressing the needs of the lower classes. Without economic growth, these demands could not be addressed without open class warfare. "For under a stationary (or even a slow growing capitalism), continued efforts of the lower and middle classes to improve their positions can be met only by diminishing the absolute incomes of the upper echelons of society" (Heilbroner 1980, 102). Harrington made a similar point. "It [the state] can, as long as production is expanding, increase the absolute living standards of the masses; it cannot change the basic structure of inequality, for that is essential to the accumulation of capital — that is, to the survival and perpetuation of the system itself" (Harrington 1976, 318). Fundamental reform that challenges the existence of the elite simply cannot be granted. It is only by continuing economic expansion that elites can maintain their positions.

It would seem, at first glance, that elite interests are not really different than those of the rest of society, but that was Mills's original point: the goals of the elite become the unquestioned goals for society as a whole. Through the socialization process and the structure of our dominant institutions, we all come to share the goals of economic growth and technological advancement. We seek to better our economic position by working harder and accumulating more. That elites benefit more by economic growth is seen by many as a necessary part of the system itself. As Dye stated, the goals of the elite seem trite and obvious. They are nonthreatening so long as industrial growth is beneficial for society as a whole.

Evidence is mounting, however, that rampant industrial growth is destroying our environment. There is a necessity to view environmental problems of depletion and pollution as manageable in a corporate-dominated society. Evidence to the contrary is denigrated or denied. Economic growth is presented as the solution to our environmental problems, not as one of the primary causes. Reforming the worst environmental abuses is performed grudgingly, but in the main, problems of the environment are dealt with by appeals for more science and technology rather than with fundamental structural and infrastructural changes. The great debates over the environment between the technological and ecological world views are not conducted purely in the realm of reason and science nor are they unaffected by structural interests. Given the stakes of the debate as well as the authority of structural elites in modern industrial societies, that is very dangerous.

In addition, evidence is also mounting that industrial growth is incompatible with traditional structures as well as with many human values. We cannot do one thing. There is a social and cultural cost to industrial intensification, a cost that is becoming increasingly difficult to deny.

4

Economic Rationalization

The structural institutions of society — family, education, religion, government, and the economy — are all interrelated, but although there are reciprocal effects among the institutions of society, the economy is the most basic. The way that a society is organized to produce and distribute goods and services is the crucial determinant in the way that other institutions are organized. In this chapter I will describe the wave of rationalization that recently began in the American economy and is spreading to all sectors of the social structure. As we will see, this new wave of rationalization has profound effects on the entire sociocultural system.

CAPITALISM

In order to grasp the extent of changes in the American economy since World War II, it is useful to describe capitalism as an "ideal type." Although America is not a purely capitalist economy (although it is usually regarded as the most capitalistic nation on earth), a description of capitalism as an ideal type will allow us to assess recent changes in the economy more accurately. There are four essential ingredients of ideal capitalism: private ownership, pursuit of profit, competition, and laissez-faire. Under ideal capitalism there is no public ownership of any potentially profitable activity. Individuals are encouraged to own the means of production (factories, vehicles, and other machinery), financial institutions, and service organizations.

The pursuit of profit is the second essential ingredient. By encouraging individuals to maximize their personal gain, they will intensify production (build more factories, grow more grain), which benefits society as a whole. This is done by providing jobs, goods, and services to the wider society.

Competition among the producers of goods and services is the linchpin of the system. It is through competition that quality is promoted and costs are kept in check. Producers of goods or providers of services must provide the highest quality at an acceptable cost or their competitors will take business away from them. This "invisible hand" of competition, which causes the inefficient to fail and the efficient to succeed, assures high quality goods at the lowest possible price. The invisible hand of competition, according to the ideal-type, makes capitalism self-regulating.

The final element is a government policy of laissez-faire (to leave alone) capitalism. Government must allow the market place to operate without hindrance; there must be a minimum of government regulation (or interference) in the economy. The invisible hand of competition requires that the losers be allowed to fail and the winners to become as large as is efficiently possible. If left unhindered by government regulation and interference, according to the theory, capitalism will provide the greatest good for the greatest number of people. The "greatest good" refers mainly to the greatest economic good — high quality goods and services, substantial employment opportunities, acceptable costs, and the general material progress of society. More generally, the "greatest good" also refers to maximizing individual freedom and economic initiative as well.

The American economy, however, has never been one of ideal capitalism. There has always been widespread recognition (although by no means universal) that the production and provision of some goods and services are best left to governments. Therefore, some potentially profitable activities are publicly owned and operated, such as the U.S. Postal Service (though recent reforms have put that bureaucracy on more of a business basis), national and state parks, the National Weather Service, municipally owned utilities, and the like. Also, there has always been some protection of domestic industry through tariff legislation, some early subsidies to railroads and other basic industries, and considerable funding for research and development in agricultural and defense industries. With these exceptions, however, until recently, American governments have generally practiced laissez-faire capitalism, particularly when compared with other capitalist nations.

The economic role of the American government has changed in the twentieth century. The federal government has become more heavily involved in giving direct subsidies to various industries (defense, oil, and automobile industries come immediately to mind) and in funding both basic science and research and development in a variety of fields — all areas that are considered essential for general economic development and security. Also, the federal government has become increasingly involved in regulating the capitalist economy. Particularly since the Great Depression of the 1930s, the federal government has been charged with regulating economic conditions through monetary, tax, and spending policies that attempt to smooth out the booms and busts to which capitalism is prone. In addition, the federal government has set up numerous regulatory commissions (with varying degrees of success) that attempt to head off some of the potential abuses of workers, the environment, and consumer product safety. Finally, again since the Great Depression, the government has expanded its role in providing social services and financial aid to those who have been dislocated by economic change or excluded entirely from economic life. This expansion by government into economic regulation has occurred as the market economy has failed to regulate itself economically, environmentally, or socially (that is, humanely or decently). The advocacy of expanded government involvement in the economy has come from two sources. The first is from people who seek protection from some of the worst abuses of the market economy; the second is from the business community itself.

The Rise and Fall of Oligopoly

Karl Marx pointed out a basic contradiction in capitalist economic theory: Competition implies winners and losers. Marx hypothesized that as capitalism developed, some firms would become larger and larger as they eliminate or absorb smaller, less successful competitors. "One capitalist always kills many" (Marx 1867, 396). The result, he pointed out, would be a monopoly. Monopolies destroy the competitive foundations of capitalism. Competition is the self-regulating mechanism of capitalism. It is the mechanism that keeps quality high and costs low. However, with the formation of a monopoly there is no longer a check on individual profit-seeking. Corporations, not supply and demand, will then control the marketplace. They will determine what is an acceptable price and what is acceptable product quality. In this particular prediction, Marx was essentially correct.

By the turn of the century many markets in the American economy were dominated by huge corporations, which, contrary to classical economic theory, control demand rather than respond to the demands of the marketplace. By the second decade of the twentieth century, many Americans recognized this problem and, through such political movements as the populists, progressives, and Theodore Roosevelt's Bullmoose campaign, advocated government intervention to "bust the trusts." As a result, the Sherman Antitrust Act and other laws were passed to prevent the development of monopolies. In the course of the twentieth century, these antitrust laws have been used to break up Standard Oil Company, the NBC Radio network, and several other large conglomerates. They have also served as part of the business environment for many American firms that seek approval from the Justice Department for proposed mergers. However, these laws are relatively weak and open to interpretation. Their level of enforcement depends on the sympathy of specific administrations, and, although they have been somewhat successful in preventing the formation of monopolies, they do not prevent the formation of oligopolies. An oligopoly exists when four or fewer firms supply 50 percent or more of a particular market. An oligopoly performs much like a monopoly.

It would be misleading to suggest that the entire American economy was dominated by oligopolies. Some sectors of the economy, such as retail marketing and clothing, have been (and remain) intensely competitive. Even among manufacturing industries, tool and die makers, part suppliers for the large auto makers, and others have enjoyed the benefits of competition (and the smaller profit margins that go with that benefit). It is also necessary to point out that laborers in the more competitive sectors, even if they are unionized, have never enjoyed the larger wages and benefits that have gone to workers in the largest oligopolies.

The American automobile industry serves as an excellent example of the process of concentration and the resulting effects of oligopoly. At the beginning of the twentieth century there were well over 200 automobile companies that competed fiercely for the American domestic market. As a result of this competition, technological innovation was high, the quality of automobiles was constantly improving, and costs were on a downward spiral. Over time, however, there were winners and losers in this competition. Many of the less successful firms went out of business;

General Motors, Ford, and Chrysler gradually bought out many others. Independent companies, such as Dodge, Cadillac, Lincoln, and Mercury, were absorbed and became divisions of the larger firms (Halberstam 1986; R. Wright 1996). By the beginning of the 1950s, America had the "big three" automakers (Studebaker and American Motors were still in business, but they were marginal players) and the effects of oligopoly began to be felt.

For corporations, competition is wasteful. It is, after all, a negative check on profits. Profits can best be maximized in an oligopoly by following the leader. In addition, because of antitrust laws, General Motors, which is about twice the size of its next largest competitor, Ford, had an interest in maintaining the appearance of competition. Ford and Chrysler, however, had an obvious interest in maintaining the status quo (R. Wright 1996; Harris 1981). Companies began to follow the lead of General Motors by becoming satisfied with their current market shares. Even in years when car sales were down, when, according to the "laws" of supply and demand prices should have fallen, General Motors would announce the latest average price increase to the press; Ford and Chrysler would soon follow suit with comparable price hikes. There was little incentive to control costs — whatever the market would bear became the rule (Harris 1981).

Layers of bureaucracy were added at corporate headquarters. In union negotiations the companies would set industry-wide contracts with labor; thus there was little incentive to keep labor costs down. In the 1960s, a significant wage and benefit premium was instituted for workers within the automobile oligopoly compared with those who worked in more competitive industries (some estimates place wages some 250 percent higher in oligopolies).

Nor was there competition among the big three in terms of technological innovation or quality. There was little technological innovation in American automobiles throughout the 1950s, 1960s, and 1970s (J. Wright 1979). The big three automakers became satisfied with cosmetic changes in design. Planned obsolescence — tailfins rather than quality — became the rule. The consumer had no place else to go. Throughout the rule of oligopoly auto executives paid lip service to capitalism and the benefits of competition in the marketplace while they practiced corporate dominance and benefited from cooperation with one another.

Part of the reason for the success of oligopolies in postwar America lies with World War II. The Arsenal of Democracy was quickly converted after the war to the production of goods for the consumer market. Most of the rest of the industrial world had been devastated by the war, and the Marshall Plan, which loaned money to wartorn European countries, was given on condition that the money be used to buy American goods. In the 1950s and 1960s, Japan and Western Europe were building new industrial plants using the latest technology, while American corporations were taking huge profits, enlarging their bureaucracies, and buying each other.

From the American experience in the postwar world the image of industrial capitalism became one of corporate giants dominating markets, padded bureaucracy, a well-paid workforce, and American preeminence in industry and technology. We told ourselves that we were competing and congratulated ourselves on how successful we were. We had secure jobs, and our children could be assured of jobs in the corporate structure. Prices might have been a little high and some of the goods a little shoddy, but we could be confident that more wages would be available next year so that we could afford a little better. Then, in the 1970s, the rest of the world caught up and, in many instances, surpassed American industries. Americans soon found out that the prevailing image of industrial capitalism was seriously flawed. The business environment had drastically changed, and corporate America was forced to compete again.

American companies, which had been protected from competition at home, did not run into serious foreign competition until the early 1970s when globalization began. The increasing importance of the global economy for America can be illustrated by the growth of the value of imports and exports combined. "No other sector of the economy has evolved so dramatically in recent decades as the international trade sector. In 1976, neither exports nor imports exceeded 7 percent of real GDP. By 1996, exports rose to 12 percent of real GDP, while imports equaled 13.6 percent" (Boustead 1997, 14). The increasing importance of international markets and the susceptibility of the American domestic market to foreign companies caught American oligopolies by surprise.

Germany and Japan, for example, became more competitive in growing world markets because of government planning and subsidies, stiff domestic competition, and the construction of more technologically sophisticated and efficient plants (Magaziner & Reich 1983; Halberstam 1986). The short-term result of globalization was that many old-line American manufacturing industries, such as steel, rubber, and textiles, faded in importance. More than 1,500 plants in these industries have closed permanently since 1975. In the 1970s in America nearly 2 million jobs were lost directly because of increased imports (Magaziner & Reich 1983).

Marvin Harris noted the initial reaction of American business: "By the mid-1970s, proud captains of American industry were down on their knees begging consumers to 'Buy American,' while pleading with Congress for treasury handouts and tariffs and quotas against foreign imports" (Harris 1981, 31). The American automobile industry, after an initial period of trying to ignore the threat and then pleading for government protection, finally began to improve the quality of its products, streamline its bureaucracies, and reinvent its production processes. As a result of globalization, many American corporations are currently downsizing their labor force, expanding managers' responsibilities with computers, replacing workers with robots or cheaper foreign labor, and paying more attention to quality and price. In large part, industry has been successful, but at the cost of serious disruption of the American workforce and American life.

TRANSFORMATION OF THE WORKPLACE

The American workplace is undergoing tremendous upheaval. Globalization has forced old-line American oligopolies to transform the ways they compete in domestic and international markets. The characteristics of the transformation are the same as those of rationalization: downsizing, rise of contingency work, tightening of coordination, human relations management, and squeezing wages. This transformation has made American products competitive in price and quality on the world market, but there has been a cost to other parts of the social system.

Downsizing

The largest American corporations have been shrinking in their efforts to compete. This reduction has been made possible by a new wave of automation, outsourcing tasks to smaller business, and other rationalizing trends. There is also ample evidence that the reduction has been made possible by increasing the workload of the employees that remain.

There is a new wave of automation, especially with computers, which is dramatically reducing the number of jobs in corporations. American corporate outlays for high-tech equipment were $100 billion in 1985, $300 billion in 1995, and were projected to be more than $500 billion by 2000 (*U.S. News & World Report* 1996, 48). The International Federation of Robotics estimated the world's robot population at 630,000 in 1991 (Rifkin 1995, 131). Industrial robots can cut materials, weld, paint, lift, package, assemble, and inspect products. The result of this trend is fewer industrial jobs and less bargaining leverage with management by the workers who remain. One estimate is that each robot replaces about four jobs; if it is kept in constant use, it will pay for itself in just over one year (Rifkin 1995). General Motors, for example, had 1,500 robots at the end of 1982 and about 20,000 by the end of 1993. "In 1993 General Motors president John F. Smith, Jr., announced plans to implement much-needed re-engineering reforms at GM plants and estimated that the changes in production practices could eliminate as many as 90,000 auto jobs, or one third of its workforce, by the late 1990s. These new cuts come on top of the 250,000 jobs GM has already eliminated since 1978" (Rifkin 1995, 130). One estimate is that robotics and other forms of automation have already reduced the number of jobs in America by about 3 million. Jobs that are susceptible to this new wave of automation are in the old-line oligopolies — steel and automobile manufacturing — the very jobs that formed the backbone of the upper-working class.

> But the elimination of jobs is not limited to the factories of the old-line oligopolies. Automation and re-engineering are already replacing human labor across a wide swath of service related fields. The new 'thinking machines' are capable of performing many of the mental tasks now performed by human beings, and at greater speeds. Andersen Consulting Company, one of the world's largest corporate restructuring firms, estimates that in just one service industry, commercial banking and thrift institutions, re-engineering will mean a loss of 30 to 40 percent of the jobs over the next seven years. That translates into nearly 700,000 jobs eliminated. (Rifkin 1995, 9)

Offices are increasingly stretching their employees' workloads through electronic means. Word-processing, electronic filing, and new communications technology are vastly improving office productivity. "Over the past ten years more than 3 million white collar jobs were eliminated in the United States. Some of these losses, no doubt, were casualties of increased international competition" (Rifkin 1995, 9), but Rifkin points out that the white-collar job loss continued even after the American economy began its recovery in the early 1990s. New technology allows employers to lower costs by replacing workers; technology is one of the primary causes of the recovery itself.

New computer and communications software is being used to increase the productivity of many professionals as well. Engineers, architects, and designers use computer-aided design software to draft and test models; presentation programs and the Internet aid professors to teach more students in a classroom and to reach community members; medical programs aid physicians to diagnose and treat their patients. By increasing a professional's ability to serve more people, computerization limits the number of professionals who will be needed in advanced industrial societies.

Rise of Contingency Work

Advanced industrial societies have entered the age of the contingency worker — the fluid, flexible, disposable worker. Replacing permanent workers with temporary or part-time employees, who are usually paid less and have no fringe benefits, is arguably the most important trend in the American economy today. Manpower Inc., the largest of the temporary worker giants, has about 2,200 offices in 41 countries; Adecco has 2,400 offices in 40 countries. Revenues reported for both companies in 1995 exceeded $6 billion (Taylor 1996). The estimates for the number of Americans who hold contingency jobs vary from 10 to 30 percent of the workforce. Most social observers agree that their numbers appear to be growing. For both large and small companies, contingency workers provide a way to remain globally competitive; to expand and contract product lines with market cycles; to avoid the costs of health care and pensions, vacations, and training; and to sidestep government antidiscrimination laws. For workers, the rules of employment vary widely. Some work part-time, others by the project or by the hour, often without any benefits other than wages.

According to former Secretary of Labor, Robert Reich, contingency workers are outside the traditional system of worker-management relations and outside the constraints of unions (Reich 1991). It is beginning to fray the social contract, which used to consist of mutual obligations and expectations between workers and their companies; a contract that rewarded employees when their companies prospered. A contract that could be kept, it now seems, only as long as the oligopoly reigned.

Tightening Coordination

Surveillience of employees

Computer systems have been designed for manufacturing to coordinate the flow of raw materials, machine time, labor, and other resources. With those systems in place, the front office can continuously monitor the production process and make decisions about inventory, manpower, and maintenance as problems occur. These systems, which were pioneered by manufacturing industries, are increasingly being used to monitor and coordinate retail and clerical work as well.

Robert Howard gave many examples of employee performance monitoring, including the following, which concerns Bell telephone operators:

> Every fifteen minutes of the day, in Bell operator offices across the country, computer terminals near supervisors' desks print out the office's complete productivity record. In a ragged, staccato tempo, these Quarter-Hour Summaries list how many operators were on duty, how many calls they handled, the average "speed of answer" — how long before an operator responds to the electronic beep of yet another incoming call. To get the productivity record of an individual employee is almost as easy. A supervisor merely keys the employee's number into the computer, and within seconds it prints out her performance for the day. (Howard 1985, 63)

Continuous monitoring of worker performance is the logical extension of managerial control of the workplace. Workers and line-managers can both be judged by their performance.

Wal-Mart was a small, regional retailer in the 1970s but became America's largest retailer in a little more than a decade. Its success is believed to be largely on the strength of an advanced computer tracking system. Wal-Mart developed its own systems to manage inventory and, via computer, ordered directly from manufacturers (Welles 1993). Apparently, even this could be made more efficient. In 1997, Wal-Mart developed a new system for managing the flow of goods from its stockrooms to the retail floor and saved more than $70 million in interest expense on its inventory in the first nine months of the year (Pressler 1997). Wal-Mart's database (on sales, inventory, and consumer buying habits) is reputed to be second in size only to the U.S. government's.

Although Wal-Mart is now widely believed to have the best computer control system in the retail industry, Eisenstodt (1993) reported that 7-Eleven stores in Japan have built their entire retail operation around computer information. Because retail floor space in Japan is extremely limited, and some 40 percent of sales are from perishable items, 7-Eleven closely monitors stock data to reduce waste and maximize profit. Each store's cash register feeds sales data, time of day, and weather conditions directly into a NEC personal computer. Clerks enter customers' sex and approximate age through the cash register at the time of sale. From a simplified keyboard, the store manager can then call up graphs and numerical data that show which products are selling, who is buying them, and when and under what weather conditions. The computer also regulates refrigerators and air conditioning and simplifies ordering. The on-site computer is only the beginning. "At 7-Eleven's Tokyo head office, daily sales to the 5 million customers who visit 7-Eleven's Japan's stores are analyzed. The aggregate results, as well as the data from individual stores, are used by 7-Eleven Japan's 650 field counselors to help stores make more money" (Eisenstodt 1993, 44). The system appears to be extremely successful; sales per store are 30 percent higher than 7-Eleven's nearest rival.

Human Relations Management

The social science of coordinating and managing people within organizations has also advanced significantly in recent years. Bureaucracies are increasingly turning to the "human relations school" of management — with benefits, quality-of-work projects, beer busts, pep rallies, stock options, and "worker participation" — to strengthen employee commitment and managerial authority. Christopher Lasch observed:

> Research into small groups, according to McGregor, showed that groups function best when everyone speaks his mind; when people listen as well as speak, when disagreements surface without causing "obvious tensions"; when the "chairman of the board" does not try to dominate his subordinates; and when decisions rest on consensus. These precepts, which by this time had become the common coin of the social sciences, summarize the therapeutic view of authority. The growing acceptance of that view, at all levels of American society, makes it possible to preserve hierarchical forms of organization in the guise of "participation." It provides a society dominated by corporate elites with an antielitist ideology. . . . Therapeutic forms of social control, by softening or eliminating the adversary relation between subordinates and superiors, make it more and more difficult for citizens to defend themselves against the state or for workers to resist the demands of the corporation. (Lasch 1979, 314–315)

By becoming paternalistic, the system of authority is disguised; opposition to management (or government) becomes more difficult to organize.

The object of the human relations school is to give workers the illusion that they have control over their work lives and that the management team is caring and concerned in order to engender loyalty and commitment to the organization. Howard characterizes the human relations school this way: "Let people feel in control without actually giving up your own power. Provide them with a pretense of participation in decisions that in fact are beyond their influence and control. Elicit the energy and engagement of close personal relationships, but make sure those relationships always remain contingent on 'usefulness' and performance. And don't ever become so close or committed to any particular relationship, any particular person, that it becomes an obstacle to exercising your authority" (Howard 1985, 128). In the human relations school, management becomes an elaborate manipulation of workers.

Capital Flight

Corporate America has an additional tool that it uses to maximize profit in the new global market: investing in overseas plants. Investment decisions are made on the basis of profit potential. Money goes where it earns more money. Although these decisions may be profitable for the corporations and their stockholders, they can be destructive for workers, families, suppliers, and local communities. Corporate capital is invested overseas to increase profits, chiefly through cheaper labor and less restrictive government regulations of the environment, employment rules, and worker safety. For example, the average weekly wage of an American assembly-line worker is about $640, including wages and benefits. In Mexico the same labor costs are about $50 a week.

Another type of capital flight occurs when corporations use their profits to purchase other companies rather than expand and modernize their existing plants. These mergers have three major consequences: an increase in the centralization of corporate capital and decision making; an increase in the power of corporations over workers, unions, and governments; and a decline in the number of jobs. The recent wave of mergers around the world is causing a downsizing in the American and global workforces. Tom Abate writes of merger activity from April to June 1998: "The six biggest corporate mergers in history have all occurred in the past three months. Investment banker Paul Deninger put that in perspective. 'It would be like six batters busting the home run record in the same season,' said Deninger, who tracks mergers for Broadview Associates" (Abate 1998, D1). (Only two batters broke Roger Maris's record.) Among the recent deals: Travelers Group bid $72.6 billion for Citicorp, NationsBank bid $62 billion for BankAmerica, Daimler-Benz bought Chrysler for $39.5 billion, AT&T has offered $60 billion for TCI cable, Bell Atlantic is offering $52 billion for GTE, and SBC is offering $62 billion for Ameritech (Abate 1998). The word among corporations is that size matters. "The reasons aren't mysterious. Technological change, deregulation, and globalization are driving many industries to consolidate" (Miller 1997, 279). By merging with former competitors, many companies can consolidate duplicate divisions (and thus reduce overall employment) in order to increase the bottom line of both businesses.

Squeezing Wages

A final method of rationalization to improve the bottom line is to put tighter controls on paychecks and benefits. One indication that this is taking place is that median family income in America, as measured in constant dollars, has not risen appreciably since the early 1970s. The average private industry wage in 1970, in constant 1982 dollars, was $8.03. By 1997 it had dropped to $7.55 (*Statistical Abstracts* 1993, table 667; *Statistical Abstracts* 1998, table 692). This is not to suggest that all wages are squeezed equally. The ratio of salaries of America's chief executive officers to the average American worker has climbed from 41:1 in 1973 to 225:1 in 1994 (*U.S. News & World Report* 1996, 47). "Fully three fifths of all households in 1994 did not even keep up with inflation . . . while the top 5 percent were awarded a $56,000 pay raise — even after adjusting for inflation — to $183,000" (*U.S. News & World Report* 1996, 47–48). Another indication of stagnating wages (although this would also be confounded with the rise in consumerism) is in the massive growth of credit card debt. In an effort to maintain a middle-class lifestyle, total consumer debt grew from $350.3 billion in 1980 to $777.3 billion in 1991 (Ritzer 1995, 7). The squeeze on wages, many economists and sociologists warn, is eliminating a good deal of the foundation of the middle class.

More than a quarter of the workforce are now in poverty, earning less than $15,000 a year (Bernstein 1996). Blacks and women are far more likely to be at the bottom of the income distribution curve than are white men. Younger and less-educated workers also fare worse than their older, more educated counterparts (Gittleman & Joyce 1995). Income inequality, or the gap between high earners and low earners, grew in the 1980s in America (Rose 1996; Gittleman & Joyce 1995). In recent decades, upward income mobility on the economic ladder has slowed dramatically; incomes are declining for an increasing proportion of Americans (Rose 1996).

New longitudinal research on social mobility — research that follows individuals, families, and households over time — indicates that the American stratification system is hardening. In the past, longitudinal data on income mobility have been misleading. First, there is a problem in terms of the age groups that were initially studied. Younger age groups are likely to show strong mobility as they enter the labor force and start their careers. Older people are likely to demonstrate the effects of retirement, when people decrease their incomes and downward mobility is common. Studies that measure social mobility on the basis of income changes between two years pick up on a considerable fluctuation in income from year to year — say, a period of unemployment that lowers income in one year but recovers in the next — and mistakenly assert that mobility has occurred. In order to get around these problems, Stephen J. Rose, an economist at the Department of Labor, took a sample of people who were 24 to 48 years old in the late 1960s and followed them over ten years until they were 34 to 58 years old in the 1970s. He also followed a group with similar age characteristics in the 1980s. In order to address short-term income fluctuations, Rose stratified his sample on the basis of their average earnings for ten years. He then compared three-year averages, 1967, 1968, and 1969, with 1977, 1978, and 1979, respectively. For the 1980s, he compared the three-year averages in 1977, 1978, and 1979 with 1987, 1988, and 1989, respectively.

For the 1970s, Rose found that 21 percent of adults ages 34 to 58 had lower family inflation-adjusted incomes at the end of the decade than they did at the beginning. In the 1980s, he found that income losers had jumped to 33 percent. He concluded that the incomes of one out of three families actually declined in the 1980s. Rose also found that in the 1970s, people of all incomes had about the same chance to move up the economic ladder. In the 1980s, however, those with more education or who started out being higher earners at the beginning of the decade were more likely to move up the economic ladder than those who had less education or started off at a lower point on the income scale.

As one might expect with all the reports of downsizing, job stability has also changed between the two decades. Rose measured job stability by summing up the number of job changes over each decade. He defined strong stability as a worker changing jobs at most once in the ten years; medium stability as two or three job changes in the ten years; and weak stability as four or more job changes in a decade. "It turned out that in the 1970s, 67 percent had strong employment stability. Some two out of three changed jobs at most once. Only 12 percent had weak stability or changed jobs four or more times. In the 1980s, only 52 percent were strongly stable, compared with 67 percent in the 1970s. Those with weak job stability rose from 12 percent to 24 percent. . . . This supports the notion that downsizing has increased and something has seriously changed in workplace relations" (Rose 1996, 6–7).

Several have remarked that the extent of social mobility (up or down) varies with class, race, and education. Bernstein summarizes recent U.S. mobility research: "As the economy stratified in the 1980s, workers at the bottom became less likely to move up in their lifetimes. At the same time, upward mobility is increasing for some higher-end professional and college-educated workers whose skills remain in high demand" (Bernstein 1996, 86). In general, the lower a group's average earnings are, the lower is the likelihood that individuals from that group will experience upward mobility. Thus blacks, women, young people, and the less educated have a harder time rising out of poverty than do older, more educated, white males. In addition, these same groups are more likely to experience downward mobility and have much more difficulty than older, better-educated white males of staying in the upper income ranges (Gittleman & Joyce 1995).

Corporations view labor as a cost. They will robotisize, computerize, send jobs to Third World countries, or take most any other action to maintain or increase profits in the short term. This should not be viewed as a criticism of "evil" chief executive officers and managers; it is the purpose of the corporation — the reason it is in business. In order to compete in world markets, companies will continue chipping away at costs by stripping away benefits, automating, cutting the workforce, and substituting contingency workers for full-time workers. Skilled contingency workers will do very well; the majority of unskilled, however, will lose income, benefits, and job security. Manufacturing jobs that remain will be of two types — those that require a skilled work force to program, maintain, and monitor the machines that do the actual labor; and marginal manufacturing jobs that cannot be computerized or profitably sent overseas. Service jobs will predominate; some of these will be of the professional and managerial class, but the bulk of service jobs will remain low-skill, low-pay, labor-intensive occupations.

IRRATIONALITY FACTOR REVISITED

Multinational corporations are the primary economic entity in today's global market. They change the balance of power between capitalism and the state. By internationalizing production, corporations can seek the lowest wage levels, taxes, and tariffs on their exports. Multinationals have more leverage with governments; they can threaten to lay off workers or move jobs to other countries if they do not get favorable treatment, such as tax breaks or relaxation of worker safety or environmental regulations. The public debate over corporate environmental policy is already full of reference to fears that multinationals will take their business elsewhere if a state becomes too restrictive. By too restrictive, I mean acting in the interests of society as a whole rather than in the interests of the corporation.

All of these strategies, which are being pursued by America's private bureaucracies (indeed, by private bureaucracies throughout the world) are highly rational, in Weber's formal or technical sense of the term. It makes good corporate sense to cut labor costs by employing robots instead of people; by sending jobs to Third World countries where labor is cheaper and government regulations are less stringent and costly; by using contingency workers; and by tightly coordinating the actions of employees. In the short term, profits will rise and budgets will be met, but it is irrational in Weber's substantive sense of the term. The long-term consequences on the market, as company after company rationalizes to reduce its labor costs, will be to seriously weaken the very foundations of the industrial system itself. If globalization follows the pattern that was established in the development of national industries, over time we would expect fewer producers as the inefficient go under and a return to oligopoly, but oligopoly on a worldwide scale, with fewer national controls on industry as governments compete for business.

However, the increasing bureaucratization and rationalization is having an effect on not only the economy and the quality of our work life but also our community, family life, and other traditional institutions. (Traditional in the relative sense of the term, that is, institutions that are guided by goals and values that are not necessarily congruent with economic profit.) Rationalization, as Weber said, becomes a habit of thought. The techniques of rationalization, having proved so successful in reviving American business, are now spreading to other institutions of our social structure. In the past, goal-oriented rational behavior in these institutions (such as activities designed to attain productivity and efficiency) were tempered by traditional, emotional, and value constraints; many institutions rationalize to more efficiently attain organizational goals including universities, government agencies, farms, professional and collegiate sports, political campaigns, entertainment and news media, health care systems, criminal justice systems, and social service agencies. All of these institutions (and others) are using rational techniques to streamline their operations to more efficiently attain the goals of the organization itself. These goals, which are consistent with rationalization, are almost exclusively defined in quantitative terms. In addition, the increasing use of rational techniques has caused traditional and value constraints on social behavior to erode.

Millions of women have joined the outside labor force, which represents a marked increase in the division of labor. This increasing division of labor has real consequences. In Chapter 5, we will explore the effects of rationalization on both the home and the community and the impact this is having on our private lives. Then, in the two chapters that follow, the rationalization of health care, agriculture, higher education, and political campaigning will be examined in detail to demonstrate the consequent erosion of traditional, emotional, and value constraints on human social behavior.

5

Erosion of Commitment

Sociology began as a reaction to the industrial revolution, which was uprooting people from the countryside and concentrating them in cities. Wealth and power were being concentrated in a new class of entrepreneurs, and there were few traditions to check that power. The French Revolution and its aftermath of terror and dictatorship also had a profound affect on the development of sociology. Early sociologists came to view the two revolutions as connected — a part of a general transformation of the old order (Kumar 1978). In their concept of the transformation, industrialization was associated not only with the transformation of the productive forces of society through technology but also with an enlargement and centralization of power (bureaucratization), urbanization, secularization, increasing division of labor (specialization), the rise of individualism, the demographic transition, and a decline of community and connectedness (a rise of alienation and anomie). All of these trends were seen as an interrelated package of social, cultural, and political changes that were associated with industrialization (currently, sociologists speak of the social and cultural package associated with industrialization as "modernization").

The perceived interrelationship of elements in this industrial package varied in what sociologists identified as the central problems of the emerging society. Marx and Weber, for example, were primarily focused on the centralization of power and authority in the new society, as well as its tendencies toward dehumanization. Comte and Durkheim were preoccupied with the disintegration of the old social order and the need to reintegrate society along new principles of social organization and morality. It was Durkheim's concern with the weakening of the social bond that provides the theme for this chapter.

Emile Durkheim elaborated the cause and effects of weakening group ties on the individual in his two works, *The Division of Labor in Society* (1893) and *Suicide* (1897). According to Durkheim, traditional cultures experienced a high level of social and moral integration, there was little individuation, and most behaviors were governed by social norms, which were usually embodied in religion. By engaging in the same activities and rituals, people in traditional societies shared common moral values, which Durkheim called a collective conscience (modern sociologists would call them the norms and values of society). In traditional societies, people tend to regard themselves as members of a group; the collective conscience embraces individual awareness, and there is little sense of personal options. As a society becomes more complex, however, individuals play more specialized roles and become ever more dissimilar in their social experiences, material interests, values, and beliefs. The growth of individualism is an inevitable result of the increasing division of labor, and this individualism can develop only at the expense of the common values, beliefs, and normative rules of society — the sentiments and beliefs that are held by all. With the loosening of these common rules and values we also lose our sense of community, or identity with the group. The social bond is thereby weakened and social values and beliefs no longer provide us with coherent, consistent, or insistent moral guidance.

Although the diversity of norms and values has the potential to liberate the individual from tradition and the hierarchies of family, church, and community, the diversity also creates problems. According to Durkheim, if an individual lacks any source of social restraint she will tend to satisfy her own appetites with little thought of the possible effect her actions will have on others. Instead of asking if this is moral or if my family would approve, the individual is more likely to ask if this action meets her needs. The individual is left to find her own way in the world — a world in which personal options for behavior have multiplied as strong and insistent norms have weakened.

Durkheim characterized the modern individual as suffering from social norms that are weak and often contradictory. A variety of groups have different values and goals that compete for an individual's allegiance. The relevance of Durkheim's insight, I believe, can be illustrated by comparing the norms on premarital sexuality for females in traditional societies with those of modern American society. (The double-standard on sexual behavior for males and females is part of our traditional morality, that is, boys have always been given mixed messages.) In a traditional setting, the strength of the bond is more intense between a young person and the relatively few groups she belongs to. The message from all social groups is virtually the same: "Don't do it." Compare this uniformity of message with the conflicting messages received by girls in modern society. In most families, the message from the parent(s) is: "Don't do it"; although the message may be mixed if a teenager has older siblings. If she belongs to a traditional church, the message is the same. Movies, television, and music video messages amount to: "Everybody's doing it" (and are probably happier as a result). Media ads are encouraging: "Just do it!" (the attempt to connect the use of a product with promises of sexual fulfillment is a widely used advertising tool). The school an individual attends, as well as "Dear Abby" are telling her: "Don't do it; but if you do, use a condom." And finally, her peer group, particularly if she has a boyfriend, is encouraging her to: "Do it." Consequently, the individual is left to her own devices; her personal desires and wants are not disciplined by consistent or strong group norms. Durkheim refers to this social condition as anomie — a condition in which individuals are given weak, inconsistent, or incoherent normative rules to follow.

The key ideas to take from Durkheim are these: An increasing division of labor weakens the sense of identification within the wider community and weakens social constraints on human behavior. These conditions lead to social disintegration — high rates of egoism, norm violation, low rates of social participation, and consequent delegitimation and distrust of authority. In the final analysis Durkheim's whole sociology revolves around this issue. His is not a straight-line evolutionary theory. In his conception, anomie and unrestrained egoism are as harmful to the individual as they are to the sociocultural system, and institutions (and individuals) react to the social disorder that results. Durkheim believed that the functional needs of society necessitate the emergence of new forms of social integration. To separate the sociologist from the reformer and the moralizer is sometimes difficult to do with Durkheim (as it can be with many sociologists). He wrote of the need for a common core of values and beliefs, whether religious or secular, that would bind us together and motivate individuals to act in an altruistic fashion. He also did research on the importance of intermediate associations that would integrate individuals more firmly to the social order and advocated their establishment along occupational lines to promote social integration. In a society characterized by a high division of labor, forces of disintegration and integration are shifting. The question I wish to address in this chapter is the state of that balance today: What is the state of the social bond in American society.

DECLINE OF TRADITIONAL FAMILIES

In general, the division of labor has increased dramatically in the modern era. More recently, in the last 30 years we have experienced an unprecedented rise in the division of labor as millions of married women joined the labor force. About 60 percent of all women over the age of 18 are in the civilian labor force today (*Statistical Abstracts* 1998, table 645). Participation by married women is almost as high. In 1990, 59 percent of married women with children under age 6 participated in the labor force (up from 30 percent in 1970) (Lugaila 1992). For women with children between the ages of 6 and 18, the rate was 74 percent (up from 49 percent in 1970). Introducing the division of labor directly into the home has numerous effects on family and community life.

In all industrial societies, the nuclear family has become the dominant form of family life. Our family system is based on strong affectional ties between spouses rather than on arranged marriages on the basis of family ties or economics. The American norm is that individuals are free to choose their marriage partners, to fall in love, and to marry whomever they choose. This emphasis on love as a foundation for marriage is unique to industrial societies. It emerged about the middle of the eighteenth century in Western Europe. Romantic love as a foundation for marriage fits well with a kinship system that emphasizes the nuclear unit. It is also compatible with the needs of a bureaucratic-industrial society. Industrial society has created an extremely mobile population, both geographically and socially. Because the family unit has been cast adrift from close ties with extended kinship systems, it has become appropriate for marriage partners to select each other on the basis of such nonutilitarian traits as love and compatibility. However, the selection process also poses a problem. Romantic love sets up some unrealistic expectations about what family life will be like. For those who have been conditioned by the media and the courtship process, few real, life-long relationships can withstand the comparison with the fantasy. More important, even for the serious-minded, romantic love can be an insubstantial foundation upon which to build a life-long partnership. Couple this insubstantial foundation with the conflicts between the present nuclear family structure and the wider society, and the wonder is not that the divorce rate is so high, but why it is not higher.

In 1998, the divorce rate in the United States was 19.5 per 1,000 married women (*Statistical Abstracts* 1998, table 156). Measures of how many marriages end in divorce are difficult to find because its timing varies and its occurrence depends on previous marriage rates. According to Norval Glenn, there has been some misinformation in the popular literature, which attempts to minimize the extent of marital breakup. Some claim that the estimate that 50 percent of all marriages end in divorce is based on crude measures of divorce (for example, baby-boomer divorces) and marriage (a smaller cohort of Generation X marriages) in recent years. Glenn notes:

> In fact, the idea that fifty percent of all marriages end in divorce comes not from such crude data but from sophisticated projections made by demographers using life-table techniques similar to, but more complicated than, those used to compute life expectancies. Such projections are not necessarily accurate predictions, but they are good summary indications of how unstable marriages were during specific periods of time. These sophisticated projections show that between 40 and 65 percent of recent marriages in the United States will end in divorce or permanent separation. (Glenn 1997, 5)

As industrialism continues to intensify, there are increasingly powerful forces for changes to the family structure. At present, there appears to be growing confusion as to how the roles of wife/mother, husband/father, and even child/adolescent are to be played. However, there are some dominant traditional expectations, which were formed in an earlier industrial era, when one wage earner (usually the male) could earn enough money outside the home to support his entire family — a situation that is rapidly passing in advanced industrial societies today. The expectation of the male in a traditional family is to be the breadwinner — to earn enough money to support the family. The traditional expectation of the female is to perform domestic chores, care for the needs of the children, and provide sexual gratification for the husband. Children are expected to obey their parents and internalize their parents' values.

The traditional roles of wife/mother and husband/father no longer fit the needs of people who live in an advanced industrial society. These traditional role expectations were part of the socialization process of children in the 1950s and 1960s — children learned how to play these roles (and how others were supposed to play their roles) through example. Consequently, the change has been very slow and painful as the people who were caught up in the shift were socialized for a very different family situation. The nuclear family is beginning to change, albeit painfully.

The most powerful force for change comes from married women entering the work force. With two breadwinners, some facets of the male role are thrust into confusion. For example, how much is the father to be involved in daily child care and household chores? Who should change the diapers, wash dishes, shop, transport children, and do other traditional female activities? Many women are finding it difficult to work in the outside labor force and perform the traditional household and motherhood roles. To date, most men have refused these tasks, which has forced many women to work outside the home and perform most of the domestic chores (Demo & Acock 1993). This situation has created enormous strains within the households of many dual-career families. An additional constraint on dual-career families is time. In order to make ends meet, many couples often work different shifts, or multiple shifts, or multiple jobs. How much time can many people actually spend together? How much time can they spend with their children?

Finally, work roles are causing people to change. We are the sum of our roles, and our roles are constantly changing in the workplace. The U.S. Department of Labor estimates that an average person will change careers three times over the course of his work life. People often change their value systems and interests with their careers. Because so many husbands and wives work, they themselves are changing. You may marry a teacher in your 20s and find yourself married to a banker in your 30s because your spouse has changed careers. "We grew apart" is one of the most common reasons given for divorce today (Gigy & Kelly 1992). In addition, although the average woman still earns substantially less than a man, women are no longer as heavily reliant on their husbands for economic support. Such women are far more likely to abandon a marriage that is not working. A husband is also much more likely to abandon a relationship when his spouse is economically independent.

The decline in birthrate has had tremendous effect on the family (National Center for Health Statistics 1995). This change can be traced to several sources: industrialism, rising costs of rearing a child, women entering the work force, and increased use of efficient contraception. In traditional societies, children are economic assets. They can contribute directly to the family unit by participating in food gathering activities at an early age, and they provide aid and comfort in old age. The long-term trend in industrial societies is to remove economic incentives to having children. The economic balance changed with the passage of child-labor laws in America early in this century and the Social Security Act in 1936. In an advanced industrial society, children become economic liabilities. Today, it costs the average middle-class family more than $200,000 to raise a child to the age of 18 — a costly decision for any couple, and one that is not likely to be made in the affirmative too often if a couple values other things in life. Women who enter the work force have also had an effect on birthrates because they are often unwilling or unable to leave the work force without affecting their earning power (in fact, this has been mediated somewhat by the use of day care at ever earlier ages). Having no or fewer children does not place a great strain on the family unit, but it does make it less stable. Not only do couples work more at their marriage if children are involved, but children are often a shared interest of the couple as well.

Day care, schools, and mass media increasingly socialize the young. The values of parents must now compete with numerous institutions to socialize children into their value system. These nonfamily socialization units often emphasize norms and values that counter the interests and values of parents — this is inevitable in a diverse, heterogeneous society. The loss of the "exclusive" socialization function of the family has had two major effects on the rest of the social structure. First, it is inevitable that some parents will come into conflict with their biologically mature, yet still dependent offspring. This is a particular strain on second marriages when the children are not biologically related to one of the parents. Second, by socializing children through multiple socialization agencies, we have quickened the process of social change. The family has been a conservative institution throughout human history. By socializing the next generation primarily through the family, the values and interests of the previous generation have always been guaranteed a close hearing. Socialization takes on more importance the earlier it is done and the more consistent the message is. By multiplying the number of "socializing agencies," we are sidestepping the family, and the interests and values of parents are now just one set in a multitude of values from which a child has to choose. In a world of change, parents and the elderly become increasingly peripheral in terms of having anything of value to transmit to a child. It is difficult for parents to compete with commercial messages of consumption and material success, particularly when experts in packaging design the messages. It is even more difficult for parents to compete with the implicit, yet highly seductive, images of sexuality and violence that are a part of the mass media's message. It is also difficult for parents to compete with government messages (through regulation of day care, mass media, and education) of individualism, consumerism, and multiculturalism, which are part of today's socialization process of children.

In traditional societies, adolescence is shorter than it is in industrial societies. In fact, adolescence can be viewed as a developmental stage that has evolved in industrial societies because of the need for extensive schooling. Today, the median age for men at first marriage is 26 (22.5 in 1970); it is 29 for women (20.6 in 1970) (*Statistical Abstracts* 1998, table 159). Some 45 percent of men and 31 percent of women are not married by their twenty-ninth birthday, and age at first marriage continues to increase in the United States (Saluter 1991). Some of this time length has to do with the increased time for specialized training and an economy that does not have enough secure and high-paying jobs for our youth. The result has been an unprecedented rise in the number of single women — often in their mid-20s — giving birth. In 1970, about 11 percent of all births in the United States were to unmarried women (*Statistical Abstracts* 1998, table 100); today it is nearly 30 percent (*Statistical Abstracts* 1995, table 136). This, coupled with the number of children whose parents are divorced at any given moment, means that almost 24 percent of children live in single-parent–headed households (*Statistical Abstracts* 1998, table 83). Often, only the mother is present. About 20 percent of all of America's children live at or below the poverty level (*Statistical Abstracts* 1998, table 759).

Sexual Revolution

Yet another social force that has put considerable stress on the family is the much-heralded sexual revolution. The traditional morality of American society has always restricted sexual intercourse to married partners. Religious tenets, lack of opportunity, and the fear of pregnancy limited nonmarital sexuality. Industrial societies have weakened religious dogma. The sexual revolution has also provided opportunities for adult men and women to interact; with the introduction of efficient contraception, sexual relations need not imply the prospect of pregnancy. The old prohibitions on nonmarital sexuality lost much of their logic. By prolonging adolescence, we have created a class of sexually mature people who have no legitimate sexual outlet. The prohibition against nonmarital sexuality was relatively easy to obey when the age of first marriage was 15. The prohibition began to lose much of its force when the age at first marriage was delayed until 25. There are some who have fully internalized religious and ethical values, some who can still muster the physical and psychological discipline to obey such a rule into adulthood. There are millions who cannot. The more permissive attitudes and values of modern societies regarding sexuality probably reflect, at least to some extent, the lengthening time spent in adolescence.

The sexual revolution weakens the traditional monopoly that the family had over sexuality. In a society in which sexual gratification has a cultural value, it is hardly surprising that some people look outside the marriage for sexual pleasure, or, if they are unmarried, see no reason why they should be deprived of sexual gratification. Doing so endangers the marriage relationship, and has been one of the reasons for the increasing divorce rate.

Modernity has clearly put tremendous pressure on the nuclear family. Because an advanced industrial society demands a mobile work force, other kin are unlikely to be nearby to shoulder household burdens, deflect emotions between spouses, care for children and aging parents, counsel adolescents, and help each other cope. The functions of the extended kinship system have been taken over, to a large extent, by formal service organizations that are staffed by professionals who are steeped in the ideology of individualism and who have no personal stake in the marriage itself.

The modern industrial family has lost most of its former functions. The traditional family was an economic subsystem of the larger society, concerned with production, the transmission of property between generations, and with reproduction and socialization of the young. Christopher Lasch (1977) believes that the modern family unit emerged in the eighteenth and nineteenth centuries to counterbalance the growing impersonal nature of our work, government, and business relations. Lasch suggested that the family's only remaining function is that of a "haven in a heartless world." It has become the center of our emotional life, and little else. As such, it has become extremely unstable. The glue that holds most marriages together is romantic love, but romantic love is the product of courtship, which is built on fantasy, mystery, surprise, and emotion. When these romantic expectations are confronted with the garbage, diapers, and weariness after a day's work, they tend to shrivel, and when romance shrivels, millions of Americans assume that because "the thrill is gone" the marriage must have failed. When it fails to live up to unrealistic expectations of permanent (and easy) bliss, people tend to dissolve the relationship and look elsewhere (not necessarily in that order).

Given the relationship of the family to the entire sociocultural system, it is inevitable that many marriages will dissolve. At one time, divorce carried enormous stigma, but beliefs have changed to accommodate the reality of marital and family breakdown. A divorce is now much easier to obtain, and it is much less stigmatizing. The statistics undoubtedly underestimate the extent of marital breakdown because they include only partners who are formally divorced. There are probably millions more married couples who are separated or who wish that they were.

Many politicians and moral leaders (two distinctly different leadership groups, but who often sound alike) believe that they have the answer to America's family problems. They argue that a return to the traditional norms and values would slash the divorce rate and solve many other problems as well. Such a return to earlier standards is not likely to happen, at least not in response to moral preaching. The family is changing and will continue to change because society is changing, but it should also be noted that it is not in any danger of disappearing. People who divorce usually remarry, which indicates dissatisfaction with the previous spouse, not with the institution of marriage itself. Most Americans are steeped in the norms of monogamy (at least in appearance) and family life. However, given the continued intensification of the industrialization process, the family will continue to change its form in order to satisfy both the personal needs of individuals and the needs of society as a whole.

The pattern that seems to be emerging is one of serial monogamy, or the practice of entering and leaving several formal marriages. The practice is already quite common. One in every four marriages in America today involves someone who has been previously married. Divorced people usually marry again within a few years, and the more often they divorce the more likely they are to marry yet again. Also, as adults, children of divorced parents are more likely to be divorced than are children from traditional homes — it seems to be a learned behavior.

The partners in these marriages have some commitment to the institution of marriage but only a temporary commitment to particular spouses. Rather than try to make a failing marriage work, they simply move on to another one. Most children will continue to be born into some kind of family situation, but the kind of domestic units involved are fundamentally new additions to the sociocultural system. Mobile individuals who enter into and opt out of formal marriages may very well be the ideal type to populate an advanced, bureaucratic-industrial society.

RELIGION

The weakening of religion and religious ideology in modern industrial societies is related to the increasing division of labor — a process usually referred to as secularization. Industrial countries show some decline in church membership, although this decline is not as marked in the United States as it is in other countries. Some 40 percent of all Americans attend church in any given week; more than 62 percent claim official membership in a local church (Stark 1994). According to Stark's studies, secularization occurs because many of the larger religious bodies, in order to encompass more diversity within their membership, no longer present the traditional versions of the faith and begin to deemphasize the supernatural. Norms and values lose their sacred character.

However, secularization is not a straight-line evolutionary development (nor is it the replacement of religion with science!). Mainstream churches, in seeking to accommodate to the modern world, reinterpret traditions and put increasing stress on the natural world as opposed to the supernatural world. This secularization in mainstream churches is the impetus for revivals, because many church members increasingly find that the church is unable to meet their religious needs. Some members leave the churches and join sects, which seek to restore the religious traditions and absolute morality of an earlier era. These efforts are often viewed with horror by the mainstream establishment. Revivals and new religions also serve to further subdivide the population. The result is a "religious economy," in which hundreds of religious organizations (some 1,500 different denominations in the United States according to Stark) exist because they appeal to specific segments of the population.

In such a religiously diverse society, the power and social influence of religious organizations continues to weaken, as does the hold those religious ideals have over our daily lives. The result is a long-term trend toward an ever more secular society as religious ideas and ideologies become more diverse and less encompassing.

As Durkheim and others have pointed out, religion serves to commit an individual to values that often transcend narrow self-interest. Norms and values lose their sacred significance in the mainstream churches, the denominations that encompass the vast majority of the population. This is not to say that religion does not play a vital role in strengthening the norms and values of society — religious beliefs are clearly vital in controlling crime, deviance, and committing the individual to social institutions. However, as commitment to religious ideals weakens and fragments, individuals are increasingly without strong and insistent moral guidance, which encourages us to act in ways other than in the interest of ourselves.

DECLINE OF COMMUNITIES

In a 1995 article that received extensive comments, "Bowling Alone: America's Declining Social Capital," Robert D. Putnam detailed and commented on the decline of community life in America. Among the items that Putnam cited as evidence of a decline in social engagement at the local level are:

Participation in parent-teacher organizations has dropped from more than 12 million in 1964 to about 7 million now.

Weekly churchgoing has declined from 48 percent in the late 1950s to about 41 percent in the early 1970s, and has remained about the same since then.

Union membership has declined by more than half since the 1950s, which represented only 15.8 percent of the work force in 1992.

Membership in traditional women's groups has declined steadily since the mid-1960s. Since 1969, membership in the League of Women Voters is down by 42 percent; since 1964 membership in the National Federation of Women's Clubs has declined by 59 percent.

Volunteers for mainstream civic organizations have also declined. Volunteers for the Boy Scouts have declined by 26 percent since 1970; volunteers for the Red Cross are off by 61 percent from 1970.

Memberships in fraternal organizations have dropped substantially. The Lions, the Elks, the Jaycees, and the Shriners have all experienced substantial declines in memberships in the last decades.

Bowling in organized leagues has declined (by about 40 percent between 1980 and 1993), while the total number of bowlers has increased by about 10 percent.

The General Social Survey indicates that total association membership has declined by about one-fourth since 1967 across educational groups. Between 1967 and 1993, the average number of association memberships among the college-educated declined from 2.8 to 2.0. A similar decline was seen in those with a high-school education or less —both groups now average about 1 membership per person.

Roper Organization data from national samples over the last two decades reveal that the number of Americans who attended public meetings on town or school affairs "in the past year" has fallen from 22 percent in 1973 to 13 percent in 1993.

The proportion of Americans who socialize with their neighbors, according to the General Social Survey, has declined from 72 percent in 1974 to 61 percent in 1993. This is somewhat offset by a rise in socializing with friends outside the immediate neighborhood, which may reflect the increasing importance of social ties in the workplace.

Putnam also comments upon the decline of the extended and nuclear family (the decline of which is so well known he mentions only in passing) which he believes reflects the general erosion of connectedness and may serve as one of the causes as well.

In explaining the decline in social connectedness, Putnam calls in all the usual suspects. First and foremost, he argues, would be women moving into the outside labor force. This movement serves to reduce the time and energy for social involvement of a significant proportion of the population, but he also notes that the trend itself cannot easily explain the decline in social participation by men, which has been as significant as that by women. He correctly points out that time-budget studies indicate that men are not sharing household child care and chores in any significant way (particularly when women are asked the questions). Perhaps a fuller explanation would acknowledge that one of the traditional roles of women was to organize the social life of the family — this is yet another role that had to be compromised because of women's participation in the outside labor force — a role that males, yet again, have not taken up in any significant numbers.

Another possible reason for the decline in social connectedness, Putnam asserts, would be that geographic mobility disrupts social ties. Putnam points out that a number of studies have found that residential stability and home ownership are clearly associated with greater involvement in the community. However, the evidence also shows that residential stability and home ownership have risen (albeit modestly) in America since 1965, "and are surely higher now than during the 1950s, when civic engagement and social connectedness by our measures was definitely higher" (Putnam 1995, 8). I believe that the hypothesis that residential stability is related to civic involvement is still viable. The reason that more widespread home ownershp does not appear to be correlated with civic engagement today may be our measures of residential stability. On a subjective level, the tie to a geographic place seems to be stronger among earlier generations. The tie may have been weakened by the cumulative effect of mobility over the last few generations.

Other demographic factors that Putnam briefly considers include divorce, fewer children, and lower real wages. "Each of these changes might account for some of the slackening of civic engagement, since married, middle-class parents are generally more socially involved than other people" (Putnam 1995, 8). Other changes, Putnam speculates, might include those that have swept over the American economy in the last few decades. Putnam refers to the decline of local merchants, the growth of mass retailing, and the rise in the number of multinational corporations.

The replacement of community-based enterprises by mass retailing, Putnam believes, may have eliminated the physical settings for social and civic engagements.

Finally, Putnam speculates that the "technological transformation of leisure" may also be partly responsible for the decline in social ties. Recent technological trends in entertainment have served to individualize tastes, privatizing the way we spend our leisure time. Television, cable and satellite systems, the video cassette recorder, video games, personal tape players, and soon virtual reality helmets serve to isolate individuals from group forms of entertainment.

Other social trends that can also be related to the decline in social engagement and community life include the rise of the individualistic ethic, the investment of more time and energy into work, and general technological changes in transportation, computers, and cellular phone communication. The social process that I believe is most related to loss of community, however, is the increasing division of labor or specialization that prevents us from identifying with each other.

Emile Durkheim posited that the increasing division of labor weakens an individual's identification with the group and weakens the sense of shared values and outlook. However, like Comte, de Tocqueville, and Spencer before him, Durkheim recognized that the increasing division of labor caused a greater reliance on a new bond between individual and society, a bond of enlightened self-interest:

> Because the individual is not sufficient unto himself, it is for society that he works. Thus is formed a very strong sentiment of the state of dependence in which he finds himself. He becomes accustomed to estimating it at its just value, that is to say, in regarding himself as part of a whole, the organ of an organism. Such sentiments naturally inspire not only mundane sacrifices which assure the regular development of daily social life, but even, on occasion, acts of complete self-renunciation and wholesale abnegation. (Durkheim 1893/1933, 228)

Suppose this enlightened self-interest is no longer operative? Former Secretary of Labor Robert Reich makes a compelling case that the recent globalization of the economy has meant that it is no longer necessary for society as a whole to do well for elites to prosper. Individuals are no longer functionally tied to the health and welfare of their fellow citizens. Security forces, educational institutions, and other essential services can be privatized more efficiently than trying to bring public institutions up to quality standards. Community needs can be ignored without jeopardizing one's own position.

Add to this possible erosion of enlightened self-interest the hyperspecialization of individuals and the sheer size, complexity, and cultural diversity of contemporary society. The result is that acts of self-sacrifice — of submerging the narrow interest of the self to the community or broader social needs — lose their foundations. Wendell Berry also commented on this phenomenon:

> Because by definition they lack any sense of mutuality or wholeness, our specializations subsist on conflict with one another. The rule is never to cooperate, but rather to follow one's own interest as far as possible. Checks and balances are all applied externally, by opposition, never by self-restraint. Labor, management, the military, the government, etc., never forbear until their excesses arouse enough opposition to force them to do so. The good of the whole of Creation, the world and all its creatures together, is never a consideration because it is never thought of; our culture now simply lacks the means for thinking of it. (Berry 1977, 22)

Traditions, sentiments, values, and enlightened self-interest previously bound us together. These ties are loosening, and in their place we have substituted rational coordination and management of competing self-interested individuals. Chapter 6 will examine recent changes in health care and agriculture along these lines.

If the decline in civic participation were confined to involvement in local community organizations it would be cause for serious concern. However, Putnam related this decline to broader concerns such as the quality of public life and the performance of social institutions. He stated that research in such diverse fields as education, poverty, health, work, and criminal justice have linked successful outcomes to living in civically active communities. Scholars of the new democracies in the post-Communist world, Putnam pointed out, have lamented the absence of traditions of civic involvement, which was the result of widespread passive reliance on the state to provide services. Putnam suggested that civic engagement and solidarity are preconditions for self-government. He also concluded from his own study of governments in different regions of Italy that the performance of representative government varied by local norms of civic commitment. Governments were effective in areas that had higher voter turnout, greater newspaper readership, and greater involvement in clubs and organizations.

Involvement in community organizations, Putnam pointed out, benefits the community at large. It promotes communication between members of the community and provides the coordination needed for collective action.

In addition, local networks encourage individuals to identify with the broader community, thus lessening the incentives for the opportunistic behavior of self-aggrandizement. Finally, involvement in civic organizations promotes self-government and traditions of community collaboration that can be drawn upon for future social action. The decline of community involvement in advanced industrial societies, Putnam asserted, is a matter of complex cultural significance.

The most significant symptom of the decline in civic involvement may be in the democratic participation in local, state, and national governments. Putnam reported a decline of nearly 25 percent in voter turnout in national elections since the 1960s. Similar trends have occurred in state and local elections as well. Decline is also evident in attendance at political speeches and volunteer work for political candidates and parties. There has also been a significant increase in the number of Americans who "trust the government in Washington" only "some of the time" or "almost never," which has gone from 30 percent in 1966 to 75 percent in 1992 (Putnam 1995, 4). The decline in social trust, according to General Social Survey data, extends across all social institutions — the media, courts, labor unions, and corporations. The decline in social trust extends to other individuals as well. In 1960, according to Putnam, 58 percent of Americans indicated that "most people" could be trusted. This proportion fell to 37 percent by 1993.

Putnam noted one significant "countertrend" in the form of new membership organizations. Such groups as the Sierra Club, the National Organization for Women, and the American Association of Retired Persons have grown exponentially during the 1970s and 1980s. Putnam noted that although these groups are obviously of "great political importance," they are of a different character than the community organizations of the past. Membership consists of writing checks for dues and receiving (and perhaps reading) the occasional newsletters. There is little attendance at group meetings and little interaction between members. The bond is simply not there. We will return to these new types of interest groups and their impact on the political life of the nation in Chapter 7.

6

Factual Regularities

The recent upheaval that began with the globalization of corporate America has spread to other sectors of the social structure as well. Private and public organizations of all types are increasingly run on the basis of rational business practices — downsizing, replacing workers with technology, augmenting professional services, outsourcing some services, and employing more contingency workers.

Government services of all kinds — military, education, mail delivery, criminal justice, and social welfare (to name a few of the most important) — are under pressure to tighten budgets. Faced with the need to control rising costs, government agencies are employing many of the same rationalizing techniques and technologies used by corporate America. Governors and presidents alike campaign with a platform to run government as a business. Legislatures are experimenting with outsourcing many government services to private corporations, such as prisons (with disastrous results for human rights), education, and welfare. Bureaucratic coordination and scrutiny are tightening. Services are being cut; providers are forced to take larger case loads; outside contracts proliferate; temporaries and part-timers become more prevalent; and increases in salary and office budgets are kept to a minimum.

In this chapter and the next I will address the spread of rationalization into some areas of social life that have been influenced by values, traditions, and sentiments other than those of rational efficiency. In analyzing these institutions according to rationalization, I intend to integrate a variety of facts and insights into a single, comprehensive framework. I wish to demonstrate that sociocultural materialism, which emphasizes the system character of sociocultural change, is an ideal framework for integrating many research findings and perspectives into a coherent structure. Society is a system; all the components fit together. The systemic structure of sociocultural materialism can serve as a preliminary guide to study how the different components of the sociocultural system interact and how the components affect human thought and behavior.

In detailing the recent rationalization of the social structure a variety of institutions could be explored. One strategy would be to simply update the work of C. Wright Mills, who applied Weber's rationalization theory to a variety of American institutions in the 1950s and 1960s. Mills was the first to explore the rationalization of war and violence. In the *Causes of World War III*, Mills wrote about the distinctive nature of violence in the modern world, with its weapons of mass destruction and high-tech weaponry:

> It is not the number of victims or the degree of cruelty that is distinctive; it is the fact that the acts committed and the acts that nobody protests are split from the consciousness of men in an uncanny, even a schizophrenic manner. The atrocities of our time are done by men as "functions" of social machinery — men possessed by an abstracted view that hides from them the human beings who are their victims and, as well, their own humanity. They are inhuman acts because they are impersonal. They are not sadistic but merely businesslike; they are not aggressive but merely efficient; they are not emotional at all but technically clean-cut. (Mills 1958, 83–84)

In the 1960s, Stanley Milgram demonstrated that men are all too willing to inflict pain on a victim when they are ordered to do so by a superior — even when personal morality presses the individual to resist authority figures. Milgram set up a mock experiment on the effects of punishment on learning. The naive subject — the teacher — was told to administer a test consisting of a list of word pairs. Each time the "learner" answered incorrectly, the teacher was to give him a shock of increasing intensity (in 15-volt increments). Beginning at 15, the teacher would shock 30, 45, all the way to 450 volts. There were also verbal designations of the switches — ranging from "Slight Shock" to "Danger: Severe Shock"; the final three switches were labeled "XXX." Milgram's findings demonstrated that many people will obey the authority figure (in this case, an actor in a white coat with no authority over the teacher) despite the protestations of the victims. He also demonstrated that the further removed a perpetrator is from the victim, the more likely the perpetrator is to inflict violence.

The weapons of war have proliferated since Mills' time. They are now more powerful and accurate; the prohibitions on the use of weapons of mass destruction seem to be rapidly eroding. The new technology of violence puts ever-greater distance between the perpetrator of violence and the victim.

The four institutions I have selected to study, medical care, agriculture, higher education, and political campaigns, share common attributes. Each one is a significant area of human activity. Higher education is a crucial activity through which to transfer the culture to future generations. It also serves to foster the fine arts, increase our understanding of natural and social phenomena, and prepare people for the roles they will play in our complex division of labor. The importance of higher education also shows up in expenditures — more than $179 billion every year (*The Chronicle of Higher Education* 1998, 34). The importance of health care is also self-evident. In economic terms, medical care now consumes more than 14 percent of gross domestic product. Agriculture is one of our most important industries in America; not only does it feed the population, but agricultural products are one of our primary exports. The political process is not only the way we select our government leaders but also how we influence our leaders on issues and legislation. Until recently, these institutions were strongly tempered by traditional, emotional, and value constraints. The constraints guided the behaviors and thoughts of the men and women who were associated with the institutions (or enmeshed in them). The rationalization process has seriously eroded the traditional constraints in each institution. Traditional and value constraints have also been weakened by disintegration, Emile Durkheim's concept that refers to the weakening of the shared symbolic world in a society characterized by a high division of labor. In a society that is characterized by a high division of labor, whose values and traditions are universal? The only values that seem to have societywide support in industrial society are those values that promote efficiency, increasing production, and profitability. The increasing dominance of such goal-oriented rational behavior in guiding human institutions, behavior, and thought is the very definition of Weber's rationalization process.

MANAGED HEALTH CARE

The health care system in America has undergone a remarkable transformation in the last twenty years and has done so largely by rationalizing the delivery of health care services along corporate lines. In the recent past it was the doctor whose traditional and value oriented notions of altruism, professional autonomy, service, and total control over medical treatment reigned unchallenged. Now, as the health care system is being redesigned along rational lines, a physician's autonomy is being threatened.

The transformation has been mandated by the spiraling high costs of sophisticated technology, labor-intensive medical treatments, and high amounts of third-party money (private insurance, Medicare, and Medicaid) in the system. Third-party money led to spiraling costs because patients are not likely to shop around for the best medical deal, particularly when they are not directly paying the bill. Physicians and hospitals had no check on the cost of their treatment, patients were not likely to seek care elsewhere, and more tests and procedures were covered by insurance companies without question. As a result, medical costs have risen faster than the consumer price index (sometimes twice as fast) every year since the 1950s. By the 1990s, health care was one of the largest industries in America, accounting for some 14 percent of the gross domestic product. Governments and corporations (which pay a good portion of the cost of medical care) found it increasingly difficult to pay the bills, and it is now through government and corporate initiatives that medical costs have shifted to individuals through higher premiums and deductibles. A second more recent initiative has been a restructuring of health care delivery so that health care providers themselves have a stake in limiting the cost of care.

One method of cost control, which was instituted by the government in the 1980s, was the Diagnostic Related Group, through which the government (through Medicare) establishes the number of days of hospital stay warranted for specific treatments and the amount it pays for treatment. If a hospital can treat the patient for less than the established charge, or discharge the patient sooner, it makes a profit. If a hospital's costs are more than the standard charge, it loses money. Private insurers quickly followed suit. The purpose of the Diagnostic Related Group is to rationalize the delivery of hospital care. It does this partly by removing professional judgment from the physician-patient relationship and partly by providing incentives for hospitals and physicians to control costs.

Perhaps the most startling transformation of American medicine is the spread of managed health care. Managed care is an institutional arrangement whereby all medical services are coordinated by a single administration. The arrangement can vary from a single entity that owns all care and services to a coordinating body that contracts services out to several different service providers. The coordinating agency is typically a for-profit corporation, such as an insurance company, a hospital or chain of hospitals, or a group of doctors (Light 1994). Insurance companies have formed the largest managed care networks; the top five health insurance companies have increased their share of total Health Maintenance Organization (HMO) membership from 55 percent in 1988 to about 70 percent in 1994 (Meyer 1994).

Managed health care is becoming the dominant form of health care financing in the United States (Merline 1994). Enrollment in HMOs reached 50 million in 1994 and is expected to exceed 56 million by the end of 1995 (Mitka 1994c). The "doctors' dilemma" of whether to join an HMO is caused by the likely collapse of private practices as HMOs expand (Woolhandler & Himmelstein 1994). Forty-two percent of physicians in the United States have HMO contracts (Meyer 1994), and nearly 90 percent are in group practices (Mitka 1994b).

The entire hospital industry is also restructuring around managed health care and corporate medicine (Mahar 1994). Wholey, Christianson, and Sanchez (1993) found that corporate interests predominated over professional interests when HMO practices are formed. Managed care systems rely upon a number of strategies to contain health care costs.

First, they depend on primary-care physicians to be frugal with tests, surgery, hospital admissions, length of hospital stay, and referrals to specialists. "Typically, managed care plans use direct financial incentives to discourage doctors from authorizing the use of tests and referrals to specialists or hospital care. In some cases, the doctors receive bonuses at the end of the year, with the size of the bonus tied to the amount of money the doctor costs the plan. The less the doctor does in a given year, the bigger the bonus" (Merline 1994, 11; Hendren 1997).

Second, managed care systems use their marketing power to set capitation arrangements with hospitals and to fix medical fees of outside service providers.

Third, the widespread use of health service data provides for elaborate patient tracking, treatment coordination, costs, and marketing. "Using figures on differential rates of treatment, surgery, diagnosis by practitioners, hospital related infections, complications, and deaths, employers and insurers make decisions on what to pay for or where to seek services" (Birenbaum 1993, 20). These data are also used to closely monitor the medical and financial performance of physicians (Vander Veer 1997).

Fourth, managed care tends to place heavy reliance on rules and procedures to guide providers when determining appropriate care.

Fifth, most managed care plans have in-house review committees or review companies to review clinical decisions. "Nurses employed by a review company — Value Health Sciences, for instance — match up symptoms with proposed treatment regimens. When a match occurs, approval is granted to provider and patient that the procedure will be paid for by the insurance company. If there is no match, a referral is made to a physician advisor employed by the review company. A negotiation process between the clinician and the adviser usually follows on the heels of the denial of authorization, a time consuming and often irritating process" (Birenbaum 1993, 21).

Sixth, managed care systems set primary care labor loads. Nurses, technicians, and aides are reporting huge caseloads. One indication of this is that HMOs average about 1 physician for every 800 enrollees; the average in the United States is 1 physician for every 400 patients (Woolhandler & Himmelstein 1994). In a 1997 Associated Press article on Columbia/HCA Healthcare Corporation, John Hendren detailed the firing of an obstetrician in Tennessee who generated only $1 million in patient fees the previous year. The physician was given a choice: a pay cut from $240,000 to $170,000 or leave (he left). The constant corporate monitoring of performance plus the pressure on health care workers to increase their patient load are all designed to increase the bottom line of the corporation.

Seventh, computer and communications technology are being used to further extend physicians' expertise and control costs. Hundreds of experimental telemedicine programs have been started around the country, largely because of their lower costs. "With a nurse in the patient's home, the video is beamed to the doctor through a camera-equipped laptop computer and telephone lines. . . . And when a 47-year-old immigrant laborer's leg was mangled in a chain saw accident in 1995 near Fort Worth, the employer saved transportation and other costs, Graves said. Columbia orthopedic surgeon James Heerwagen, more than 40 miles away in Lewisville, walked an on-site health-care worker through the draining and closing the wound" (*The Orlando Sentinel* 1997, C1, C9).

Eighth, delaying treatment or denying patients access to newer tests, procedures, or expensive drugs is yet another strategy for controlling costs (Merline 1994). These delays and denials can stem from complicated rules, cumbersome bureaucracy, and pecuniary interests of the third-party payer.

With the focus on the bottom line, many are concerned that patient care will suffer (Meyer 1994; Hendren 1997). New administrative bureaucracies have created high overheads in the form of managers and their salaries (which can run into hundreds of thousands of dollars per executive). The elaborate data gathering and analysis for monitoring and marketing, costs for generating documentation by providers, and fees for review agencies also take money away from direct patient care. Money is also taken from patient care to feed corporate profits (Light 1994; Birenbaum 1993). Recently, there has been evidence that the cost of health care in the United States is again rising faster than the cost of other services — an indication that managed care is not meeting its primary goal of efficiently providing medical services.

Furthermore, there is still the irrationality factor. "Health plan administrators demand industrial 'efficiency' at the level of each doctor/patient encounter, producing chaotic inefficiency for the health care system as a whole" (Woolhandler & Himmelstein 1994, 265). There are many horror stories of the obsessive focus by HMOs on profits (McCormick 1994; McCarthy 1994; Hendren 1997) and patients being denied basic medical care. Among the recent stories are "Cancer Patient Dies from HMO Delays," "HMO Delays Bone Marrow Treatment and Patient Dies," and "HMO Denies Hospital Care for Aneurysm, Then Rehabilitation Costs" (Hendren 1998, 7B). The structure of managed care promotes profits over patient care. Woolhandler and Himmelstein have a similar take on the problem: "The managers and financiers who increasingly dominate care are not bad people (if so, we'd need only replace them); they're just responding appropriately to a system that demands misbehavior: Put profits before patients or go under" (1994, 206).

INDUSTRIALIZATION OF AGRICULTURE

I have a deep fondness for the work and philosophy of Wendell Berry, as do many people from Kentucky. A writer of short stories, essays, and poetry, Berry has developed a holistic philosophy that, although deeply personal and often poetic, is consistent with the ecological-evolutionary perspective in this book. Berry's essays often focus on the same themes and processes as the social studies, although, obviously, they grew out of a different tradition. My critique is, therefore, twofold: to illustrate the perspective of sociocultural materialism through a discussion of *The*

Unsettling of America by Berry (1977) and to introduce Berry's perceptive critique and analysis of industrial agriculture to students of society. Although his focus is on agriculture, Berry believes that the industrialization of the American farm is but a part of the larger process, one that has similar effects in other parts of the social system.

The heart of Berry's analysis centers on our relationship with the earth. He believes industrial agriculture is an extractive exploitation in which maintenance and care for the land has given way to short-term production goals. The use of large-sized equipment has forced many farmers to give up contour plowing and wind breaks as soil conservation practices. The high amounts of chemicals have caused an inevitable spillover into the wider environment. Agricultural industrialization has come about at the expense of more pollution and environmental depletion. This type of agriculture, based on nonrenewable resources, is sustainable only as long as topsoil, water, and oil remain plentiful and pollution is within tolerable limits. Berry believes that if we continue to intensify production, we will exceed these limits.

Berry's work and that of others has set off a great debate over sustainability. The literature is rife with articles that detail depletion and environmental pollution in agriculture and just as much literature minimizes the problems. Solutions to these problems advocate either a return to earlier agricultural practices or further technological innovation to minimize environmental disruption. I now examine the connection between industrial agriculture and its effects on the wider sociocultural system.

Intensification

The industrialization of agriculture began in the early twentieth century. It consists of applying scientific and business practices to food production and includes the following specific practices:

- highly specialized farms that produce a single crop or animal;
- oversized mechanical equipment that tills soil, plants seeds, or harvests acres of land in minutes;
- liberal applications of chemical fertilizers, pesticides, and herbicides;
- large amounts of water for irrigation;
- scientifically manipulating seeds to increase their resistance against diseases and to increase yields; and

raising specially bred livestock in large numbers through the unsparing use of designer feeds, mechanized feeding and waste removal, and drugs.

These innovations have been used to both replace human labor on the farm and to maximize productivity. Further intensification of plant and animal production can be expected as advances are made in genetic engineering.

Intensification in agriculture can be measured in the growth of production of various products. Grain production (mainly wheat, rice, and corn), grain yields per hectare of land, and meat production all indicate that agricultural productivity has risen dramatically around the world since 1950 (Brown, Kane, & Roodman 1995). For example, world grain yield rose from 1.06 tons per hectare in 1950 to 2.58 tons in 1992, an increase of 143 percent (Brown, Kane, & Roodman 1995, 27). Growth in meat production has been even higher; in 1950, the world produced 46 million tons of beef, pork, poultry, and mutton. In 1992 the total was 179 million tons, an increase of 289 percent (Brown, Kane, & Roodman 1995, 31). Although growth in each commodity has been slowing in recent years, the rise in food production has so far kept pace with population growth.

The use of fertilizers has shown a short-term decline in the last ten years — perhaps because of rising prices, changing patterns of government subsidies, and limits on the ability of plants to respond to heavier applications. Nonetheless, artificial fertilizer, which is highly energy intensive to manufacture, has been one of the two main factors in high yields since mid-century (Brown, Kane, & Roodman 1995, 43), and the growth in the use of fertilizer since 1950 has been extraordinary. Water is the other main factor in increased agricultural productivity. "The growth in world irrigated area during the third quarter of this century was extraordinarily rapid, averaging some 3 percent a year" (Brown, Kane, & Roodman 1995, 42). This growth, too, has slowed down in recent years because it has approached or exceeded its sustainable limits.

In order to attain this productivity increase, the amount of energy invested in food production has risen dramatically. Traditional agriculture used about one calorie of energy (usually in the form of human and animal labor) to produce ten calories of food. David Pimental of Cornell University has shown that to produce and deliver one can of corn, which contains 270 calories, now requires 2,790 calories of energy, almost all fossil fuel, to power machinery and manufacture pesticides, chemical fertilizers, and transport the food to the market (Harris 1977). "The production of beef now requires even more prodigious energy deficits: 22,000 calories to produce 100 grams (containing the same 270 calories as in the can of corn)" (Harris 1977, 284). The productivity of industrial agriculture depends upon these tremendous energy deficits — deficits that can be maintained only as long as fossil fuel remains abundant.

Bureaucratization

On the basis of its huge capital outlays, industrial agriculture promotes the concentration of farmland in order to achieve economies of scale, which has led to the decline of farm families and communities and to the rise of agribusiness. Each year since World War II, there have been fewer farms, and farms have become larger. Berry contrasted the industrialization of the American farm with forced collectivization in the former Soviet Union. In the Soviet Union, the central government forced entire villages into collective farms. In Washington, the slogan in the Department of Agriculture was "Get big or get out," and governments at all levels pursued policies that promoted the growth of the American farm. The only difference, Berry said, was in the method. The Soviets used military force; in the United States the force was economic. The people who have been moved off the land often gravitate to urban areas, many to become a permanent underclass, excluded from participating in modern society. It seems possible, then, that industrial farming has not only destroyed farming communities but also has contributed to the disintegration of urban life as well.

The concentration of American agriculture continues. Changes in farm technology have reduced the emphasis on labor-intensive agriculture, thus reducing the need for farm workers and even farmers themselves. Because new technologies are so expensive, their use is not efficient on small farms; consequently, they fuel a process of concentration as farm owners are forced to sell, while others invest in the technologies and expand. This process, which was already well advanced by the 1960s, is illustrated in U.S. government statistics: From 1963 to 1993 farm employment fell by half (from 4,364,000 employed workers to 2,041,000). In that same period, the number of American farms dropped from 3,572,000 to 2,065,000 (a 42 percent decline); the average farm size increased from 322 acres to 474 acres (an increase of 47 percent); and production soared almost by half (Ilg 1995). "Farms with annual sales of more than $500,000 account for 1% of the number of farms, 30% of the total agricultural production and 45% of net farm income" (*The Economist*, 1993, 73).

The driving force behind the growing concentration of agriculture has been the technological developments that force farmers either to grow in size or get out of agriculture completely. In order to compete, farmers need to increase the size of their farms. "The result is a farm sector with fewer operators and still fewer laborers and the role of farming in small-town America has become much less significant" (Ilg 1995, 5).

Structural Feedback

Berry convincingly demonstrated that the intensification of agriculture has been promoted by a collaboration among bureaucrats — agribusinessmen, agriscientists in universities, and bureaucrats in government. It is their interests, ambitions, and goals that have determined the direction of agriculture. As such, it has been the interests of merchants, industrialists, academic careerists, and government workers that have guided the industrialization of the farm; "who have promoted so-called efficiency at the expense of community (and real efficiency), and quantity at the expense of quality" (Berry 1977, 42).

Of the three bureaucracies that have been promoting the intensification of agriculture, Berry heaped the most scorn upon agricultural professors: "The careerist professor is by definition a specialist professor. Utterly dependent upon his institution, he blunts his critical intelligence and blurs his language so as to exist 'harmoniously' within it — and so serves his school with an emasculated and fragmentary intelligence, deferring 'realistically' to the redundant procedures and meaningless demands of an inflated administrative bureaucracy whose educational purpose is written on its paychecks" (Berry 1977, 148). Professors, according to Berry, define agriculture in purely commercial terms. Their goal is to promote an agricultural system that provides food as efficiently as possible (meaning quickly, cheaply, and with minimum human labor) as well as to create a market for agricultural machines and chemicals.

Agribusiness and chemical firms are increasingly dominating agricultural research. "Like the sorcerer's apprentice, the industry spends vast amounts of effort and money putting right the things it put wrong in the first place. . . . The research that private industry does, and which it solemnly publishes in the learned journals, is geared towards telling us the obvious — such as the fact that tethered pigs have high blood pressure, or that fertilizers lead to soil erosion — and then finding hi-tech solutions to those problems" (Hutchings 1989, 13–14). To advance in academe, or to make one's self marketable for lucrative jobs in other agricultural bureaucracies, Berry contends that one's research must be oriented toward agribusiness, not toward the land or the farmers who work it.

Berry was hostile to academicians because the land-grant college system was specifically instituted to promote the interests of independent farmers, who Thomas Jefferson believed were the backbone of democracy. The academics in agriculture, like experts in many bureaucracies, defined their goals in quantitative, measurable terms. Productivity became the yardstick; values of the land, the welfare of the farming people, even of the total society, were simply not considered. Partly as a result of academic research, millions of farmers and farm workers have been forced from the land and the land is rapidly becoming depleted and polluted. Consequently, bureaucracies that were originally set up to help farmers and farm communities actually pursue goals that end up destroying the very groups they are supposed to serve. Berry described the general process of the irrationality of zweckrational in words that strongly echo Weber's: "The practical, divorced from the disciplines of value, tends to be defined by the immediate interests of the practitioner, and so becomes destructive of value, practical and otherwise" (Berry 1977, 158).

Rationalization

What Berry condemned in modern agricultural bureaucracy is the obsessive focus on productivity (zweckrational or goal-oriented rational behavior) to the exclusion of all other values, emotions, and traditions. "Modern American agriculture has made itself a 'science' and has preserved itself within its grandiose and destructive assumptions by cutting itself off from the moral tradition (as it has done also from the agricultural tradition) and confining its vision and its thought within the bounds of internal accounting" (Berry 1977, 172). Like the goal-oriented behavior of other bureaucracies, those of agriculture ignore tradition, emotion (such as love for the land), and wider social values (such as care of people) in their attempts to achieve greater production. In Marx's words, "Agriculture comes to be more and more merely a branch of industry and is completely dominated by capital" (Marx 1972, 325).

Berry also perceived the corrosive effects of excessive zweckrational experienced outside the agriculture bureaucracies on the farmers themselves:

> The concentration of the farmland into larger and larger holdings and fewer hands — with the consequent increase of overhead, debt, and dependence on machines

— is a matter of complex significance. . . . It forces a profound revolution in the farmer's mind: once his investment in land and machines is large enough, he must forsake the values of husbandry and assume those of finance and technology. Thenceforth his thinking is not determined by agricultural responsibility, but by financial accountability and the capacities of machines. . . . He is caught up in the drift of energy and interest away from the land. Production begins to override maintenance. The economy of money has infiltrated and subverted the economies of nature, energy, and the human spirit. (Berry 1977, 45–46)

The structure of industrial agriculture promotes, even demands, that those who work the soil do so within the narrow goals of maximizing production, at the expense of all other values. Thus, there are family farms, such as "Salyer-American," that are increasingly run on a strict, businesslike basis, with five-year plans, international marketing executives, and computerized cost-accounting systems down to 20-acre plots to get a better grip on profitability (*The Economist* 1997, 73). "The trouble is that farming is now largely out of the hands of the farmers . . . farmers are on a treadmill that they are powerless to control. If the featherless chicken comes, farmers will be forced to breed it, or go out of business" (Hutchings 1989, 14).

Berry also described a change in the way modern people perceive the world. An individual's perceptions of the world and her place in it, Berry argued, are greatly affected by how she goes about making her living. An agricultural way of life encourages people to view their world in terms of natural cycles and rhythms. By adopting an industrial mode of production people begin to view the world as raw material to be manipulated and exploited for their own ends. Berry's analysis bears similarities with Weber's concepts of human action and the rationalization process. Both men attempted to describe the same characteristic shift in social thought and action.

Superstructural Feedback

Berry recognized the connections between the way we go about making our living, the social structure, and our values. The removal of human values and traditions from productive activity, which many would claim defines our very humanity, necessarily affects all areas of our lives. It leaves us cut off from our past, cut off from wider moral and social values, and cut off from our humanity. Berry described the connections:

It is impossible to mechanize production without mechanizing consumption, impossible to make machines of soil, plants, and animals without making machines also of people. (Berry 1977, 75)

If human values are removed from production, how can they be preserved in consumption? How can we value our lives if we devalue them in making a living?" (Berry 1977, 79)

But then it must be asked if we can remove cultural value from one part of our lives without destroying it also in the other parts. Can we justify secrecy, lying, and burglary in our so-called intelligence organizations and yet preserve openness, honesty, and devotion to principle in the rest of our government? Can we subsidize mayhem in the military establishment and yet have peace, order, and respect for human life in the city streets? Can we degrade all forms of essential work and yet expect arts and graces to flourish on weekends? . . . The answer is that, though such distinctions can be made theoretically, they cannot be preserved in practice. Values may be corrupted or abolished in only one discipline at the start, but the damage must sooner or later spread to all; it can no more be confined than air pollution. If we corrupt agriculture we corrupt culture, for in nature and within certain invariable social necessities we are one body, and what afflicts the hand will afflict the brain. (Berry 1977, 91)

A society that defines immediate productivity and efficiency as ultimate value and judges all by these standards cannot afford concern for tradition or wider social concerns.

Modern bureaucracies and modern thought (zweckrational) promote continued intensification, implying infinite industrial growth and consumption, but considering wider cultural concerns, Berry argued, leads to restraint in our pursuit of affluence. These wider concerns, however, have been weakened along with our families and communities; they are not given voice in our bureaucracies; they are not given value in our culture.

7

Widening Gyre

It should be clear by now that I am not claiming that rational planning and the efficient attainment of goals have no role in preindustrial societies — or that they should be eliminated in all of their manifestations in modern industrial life. Such claims would be ludicrous. Rational, goal-oriented behavior is part of our humanity and has always been an important part of human action. Weber wrote that there were four motivators of human action — values, emotions, traditions, and goal-oriented rational behavior. These motivators, it can be said, define our very humanity, but when social institutions and norms consistently promote and instill goal-oriented rational behavior over behaviors that are guided by values, traditions, and emotions, then rational behavior becomes dangerous to both individuals and society. Such a society could be the very definition of alienation — it attempts (sometimes successfully) to cut off the individual from part of her self and from part of her humanity. In the social order, values, emotions, and traditions restrain individuals in their attempts to satisfy personal goals (or, more dangerously and efficiently, organizational goals). In fact, we label this type of individual behavior as "unbridled." The erosion of these internalized constraints threatens civilization itself.

HIGHER EDUCATION

In 1959, C. Wright Mills wrote about social science professors who were highly specialized and overly concerned with the trappings of science — obscure theory and empiricism — rather than furthering the understanding of their disciplines and of the social whole. To further their careers, many professors rely almost exclusively on scholarly productivity (defined as counting the number of articles in proliferating journals), rather than advancing their discipline. Mills also pointed to an increasing focus on collecting grants from federal, state, and corporate sources. The ability to write and receive grants is lucrative for universities (some of which take a significant cut for administrative costs) and convenient for administrators who must measure the productivity of their faculty. This tendency among the professors has only gotten worse. In 1996, the total spent on research and development by doctorate-granting institutions was well over $22 billion (this figure excludes funding for arts, humanities, and education) (*Chronicle of Higher Education Almanac* 1998, 5). In 1998, it is now possible to write of hyperspecialized professors who try to get as far away from undergraduate education as possible. An update of Mills's critique would not have to focus exclusively on the head of the class; there are several rationalizing trends, most in the name of efficiency, that are rapidly transforming the university itself.

Internal Efficiency

Several rationalizing trends in American universities can be considered home grown — internal to the university and mirroring the goal-oriented norms of measurement, coordination, and efficiency that increasingly dominate society as a whole. They arise internally to meet the needs of the institutions themselves — the need to increase productivity and efficiency because of tightening budgets. Universities can no longer expect significant increases in state funding and are therefore forced to further rationalize their organization by controlling instructional costs, tightening coordination, cutting low-producing programs, and raising tuition and fees.

The tightening of coordination is evidenced by the rise of continuous evaluation of faculty through measures of student performance, student opinion surveys, and monitoring of professorial performance in the classroom. These reviews are conducted for purposes of merit, promotion, and tenure. This change in monitoring is part of the increase in educational bureaucracy (administrators have to administer something), and part, no doubt, is because of the general tightening of coordination and control, which is exhibited throughout society, to assure continuing productivity of the workforce. We no longer assume that professionals will perform unless they are monitored. The tenure process has come under increasing review. One proposal calls for a post-tenure review process; others call for scrapping the tenure process itself.

Courses are becoming standardized. Some of this standardization of course content was accomplished through the widespread use of textbooks, but the move to standardize curricula comes from many modern sources — accrediting boards, state agencies, federal mandates, and universities themselves. Most standardization is undertaken to promote quality and comparability across universities; apparently faculty are no longer qualified to decide on their own course content, students can no longer survive a "bad" professor, and ease of transferring credit between institutions has become a major goal of each university.

The university has seen recent growth in the power and influence of a central administration; an increasing share of resources that go toward administrative costs demonstrates this. As the sheer sizes of faculty, student body, and physical plant of a university grow, the division of labor increases and the mechanisms of coordination and control enlarge and centralize.

There are more professional educators, communicators, and budgeteers in administration instead of the more traditional administrators who came through the ranks of academia. Coming up through the ranks often meant being imbued with academic values. David Riesman (1980) indicated that most college and university presidents came invariably from the ranks and had a doctoral degree — doctorates in education were extremely rare (Riesman 1980, 1). Today, almost 22 percent of college presidents hold the Doctor of Education as their highest degree, and fully 42 percent of all university presidents come from the field of education (*Chronicle of Higher Education* 1998, 30). It seems that holding a specialized degree in educational administration (or some related field) is rapidly becoming the credential needed for higher academic administration.

Adjunct professors are increasingly relied on (contingency workers who are even more exploited than the ones in corporate America) as are graduate students (who are even more exploited than adjuncts) to teach undergraduate courses (Barkume 1998). The percentage of faculty who teach part time has increased from 30 in 1975 to 41 in 1995 (*Chronicle of Higher Education* 1998, 29).

I could only find passing reference to increasing class size, but it is consistent with my own experience and those of my colleagues at other universities. By increasing class size faculty become more productive in generating credit hours. They also tend to rely more on multiple-choice tests and other bureaucratic instruments to manage their larger classes.

One prominent rationalizing trend consists of the use of technology to increase the number of students that professors can teach. "Alternative delivery systems" (a term I picked up in Australia — we are not alone) consist of such technologies as the Internet, TV classrooms, and interactive computer laboratories. Plans in Kentucky call for the establishment of the Commonwealth Virtual University, in which courses will be taught entirely through alternative delivery systems. Courses will be conducted through public television, the World Wide Web, videotape, closed-circuit TV classrooms (which will wire campus classrooms to other sites), or simply through the mail. All of these cost-cutting trends increase the rationalization of education, tend to limit the professional wage component, and increase the profitability of the university.

Market Efficiency

Universities have proliferated in size and scope since Mills's day. It is apparent to anyone who has worked in higher education over the last 30 years that things are rapidly changing. Numerous trends in American university education are being caused by broader social and cultural rationalization: attempts on the part of universities to more efficiently meet the needs of advanced industrial-bureaucratic society. The list begins.

The health of a university is increasingly measured by growth or, at the very least, by maintaining market share. Riesman, a sociologist and advocate of educational reform through his work with the Carnegie Foundation, in 1980 identified the "student as consumer" as a primary cause of recent changes in American higher education. In response to the baby boom, public and private universities and colleges expanded and overbuilt during the 1960s and 1970s. These same institutions are now desperate for warm bodies. Riesman examined the consequences of this competition and found that it has affected universities as well as society as a whole. One indicator of the vigorous recruitment of students is the growth in the percentage of high school graduates (ages 18 to 24 years) who attend college, which has gone from 34.3 percent in 1986 to 43.5 percent in 1996 (*Chronicle of Higher Education* 1998, 19). Because the number of 18 to 24 year olds is declining, colleges must widen their net.

Individuals and institutions increasingly focus on higher education almost exclusively as a means of occupational training for individuals (and nothing more). College students are responding to real market conditions. Mark Mittelhauser wrote of the occupational reality that recent and future graduates will face: "This labor market dilemma for college graduates is not new. In fact, it has existed for more than a decade and is expected to continue. According to the Bureau of Labor Statistics (BLS), there were about 250,000 more college graduates entering the labor force each year between 1986 and 1996 than there were new college-level jobs. This number represents about 1 in 5 of the college-educated entrants to the workforce" (Mittelhauser 1998, 3). People increasingly go to college, Mittelhauser reports, because the labor market favors college graduates. They earn more, suffer lower unemployment than those with a high school diploma (the 2.4 percent unemployment rate for college graduates in 1996 was less than half the 5.7 percent unemployment rate for high school graduates in the same year). In addition, major occupations that require college-level applicants are growing faster than jobs in the economy as a whole. Part of this is the result of the changing nature of the economy. Part of it is also the result of the educational upgrading of many existing jobs.

The bulk of the jobs available for college graduates are professional specialty occupations (engineering, registered nursing, law, teaching, and social work) — the largest and fastest growing cadre of college-level jobs. The second largest category is executive, administrative, and managerial occupations. Together, these two broad groups account for more than two-thirds of college-level employment in the United States (Mittelhauser 1998).

Surveys of incoming freshmen in fall 1997 showed that people increasingly go to college to get the credentials for these jobs. Noted as very important in deciding to go to college, 74.5 percent of respondents indicated "to be able to get a better job" (the highest of any single category). The second highest percentage — 74.3 percent — indicated "to learn more about things that interest me," which is not consistent with the career orientation. (As Max Weber pointed out, human behavior is very complex and is usually motivated by a mix of rationality, values, emotions, and traditions.) The third most widely given reason was, "to make more money" (73 percent), which fits the career-orientation pattern (*Chronicle of Higher Education* 1998, 22).

This personal vocational focus is supplemented and encouraged by a political system that consistently promotes higher education as a means of economic development; an economic system that demands that higher education subsidize its training costs; and a campus system that increasingly follows corporate and government priorities. Colleges and universities are rapidly becoming worker-training centers for the bureaucratic-industrial state by selecting, sorting, and training future workers for it. This vocational focus and the attempt to maintain or increase student numbers among a declining pool of applicants has resulted in a variety of marketing and recruitment efforts.

One of the most obvious consequences of marketing to students is the proliferation of professional and semiprofessional degrees. This is accompanied by the precipitous decline of the liberal arts as a viable major, particularly in the nonapplied fields of philosophy, English, and social studies — the bulk of the traditional disciplines that used to define university education itself. (The natural sciences, which are more amenable to career and practical applications, have not suffered from these same declines.) Majors in college do not just teach a list of skills and general factual knowledge. Rather, they socialize students to the values, ideologies, and interests of the discipline (this is true of any discipline, although I would argue that the liberal arts tend to instill broader values and ideologies than do professional fields). For too many students, the liberal arts and humanities that they *may* be exposed to in their core courses are nonessential, tolerated (to varying degrees), and subordinate to their occupational major. When professors in the humanities and social studies critique society, they are often teaching to students who already have a vested interest in the status quo: junior doctors, business people, and social workers. This makes students much less playful and less willing to experiment with new ideas. It also goes a long way toward explaining why undergraduates no longer have a unique subculture.

Aggressive recruitment has also resulted in a proliferation in the number and power of professional and occupational accrediting boards, which often dictate courses and course content to the faculty. This trend is a mix of standardization to ensure minimum quality and relevance of the educational program for student consumers, and self-interest by occupational groups to restrict access and enhance employment within the profession as well as within academe itself.

Marketing to nontraditional students (older than age 25) has led to an increase in the clientele of the university. Many older students need to retrain for the ever-changing economy. This marketing strategy is part of the greater general career focus of universities. The age of students enrolled in college has climbed markedly in recent years. Today, more than 42 percent of all college students are 25 years or older (*Chronicle of Higher Education* 1998, 18).

Another attempt to expand the number of students is to increase the number of foreign students on campus or to locate satellite campuses overseas. Many have written of universities that oversell themselves in foreign markets to the detriment of the students themselves (Riesman 1980, 218–224).

Resources devoted to responding to federal and state requests for data to ensure accountability have increased. This, Riesman suggests, is often done in the name of consumer protection. Colleges and universities would apparently all become degree mills if left to their own devices by selling credentials to those who could afford them.

In order to maintain student numbers or to grow, universities have increased the amount of resources devoted to marketing the university. The costs of student marketing are rising. In 1980, Riesman pointed out that the escalation of marketing strategy was based on the irrational belief that other institutions would not follow the same strategies to increase their enrollment and thus cancel out any temporary gains in the number of students, but which renders the recruitment process far more expensive. Riesman gave a classic example of the irrationality factor: "Each director of admissions thinks his or her stratagem is unique, failing to realize that a hundred others, no less hungry and intelligent, will think of the identical devices" (Riesman, 1980, 113). The high-stakes costs of recruiting students have to be borne by students either in the form of higher tuition, larger classes, inadequate library or computer support, or ignoring maintenance of university facilities (Riesman 1980).

All of these changes (and others) can be directly related to the increase in industrialization, a consequent increase in the division of labor, and the growing function of colleges and universities in training that labor. However, there is still a little more; there is the irrationality factor, the effect of all of these changes on the educational "product" itself.

Irrationality Factor

Professors will complain about students in campus offices and in the hallways of professional meetings (where most of the real discussions take place). We complain of students who are not conversant with their culture; students who are overtly hostile toward the arts, humanities, and social studies; students who are indifferent toward politics and the governance of their society; students whose only interest (and value) seems to be the pursuit of a comfortable career. Some of this talk, no doubt, is a look back (with heavy doses of nostalgia) to the days when we were undergraduates — when we were going through the most exciting time of our lives. However, by marketing to student wants, in the form of watered-down core requirements and an emphasis on vocational education, institutions do not always give students what they need.

Evidence of the general decline in standards at many universities comes out in report after report. A Department of Education study in 1993 indicated that more than half of American college graduates could not read a bus schedule. "Exactly 56.3 percent were unable to figure out how much change they should get after putting down $3 to pay for a 60-cent bowl of soup and a $1.95 sandwich" (Leo 1997, 14). In 1995, Bruno Manno reported, "We're 'dumbing down' the curriculum and descending into ever lower levels of remediation. A 1992 analysis of college transcripts of recent bachelor's degree recipients showed that slightly over 26 percent of the recipients had not earned undergraduate credit in history and almost 31 percent had not studied mathematics of any kind" (Manno 1995, 48).

Remedial courses are offered in 91 percent of public colleges, and in 58 percent of private colleges. Some 23 percent of colleges award degree credit for remedial courses. Almost all colleges allow remedial students to take college-level credit at the same time (Manno 1995). Manno asks, "Can it be true that large numbers of students unable to do serious college-level work in reading, writing, and mathematics are able to do serious college-level work in history or business?" (Manno 1995, 48). Open admissions, Manno claimed, sends the wrong message to high schools and their students. No admission standards in college lead to no exit standards in the high schools.

Both Riesman and Manno relate the decline in standards to market relationships between the university and student. With institutions competing frantically with each other for students "faculty members and administrators will hesitate to make demands on students in the form of rigorous academic requirements for fear of losing 'FTE's — full-time equivalent students" (Riesman 1980, xiv). The erosion of the core curriculum — the number and quality of courses (often designated as general education or distribution requirements that are aimed at educating the whole person) shows this same decline in standards and rigor "since any requirement is likely to turn away prospects" (Riesman 1980, 108).

Another factor behind the decline of general standards and core curricula would be the disintegration (in Emile Durkheim's sense) of broadly subscribed cultural norms, values, and ideologies. There has been an increase in specialization at universities, which has led to multiple disciplines and special interests in campus debates about university standards. There has also been growth in the opportunities for women and minorities on the faculty and in administration. (I would argue that equality between races and sexes is part of the general rationalization process, which makes the rationalization process not all bad.)

Finally, there have been a number of academic movements — postmodernism in particular — which are hostile to the entire humanistic and scientific tradition of the West. Postmodernism emphasizes such themes as subjectivism and relativism; it rejects notions of objectivity, truth, and the validity of the scientific enterprise — all rooted in the observer, his class, race, and resulting ideology (Harris 1995). Consequently, it is now difficult to get professors to agree about what should constitute a common core and what forms of ignorance are unacceptable — what every student must know.

There is another side of the issue of declining standards. That those on top of the industrial-bureaucratic hierarchies are in need of a broad-based, traditional, liberal arts curriculum can easily be argued. In an advanced industrial society, that need may be as high as 15 to 20 percent — a figure that our best private and public colleges can supply, but it is difficult to make the same argument for the millions of technocrats, semiprofessionals, and middle managers that the private and public universities annually produce. If we assume that most of these millions are destined to serve in the middle levels of bureaucracy, or, at best, as professionals who are dependent upon both public and private bureaucracies, it could be argued that the old liberal arts disciplines are counter to the bureaucratic needs. Critical thinking (which I would define in terms of Weber's concept of wertrational — the ability to exercise rationality within a holistic context) is not in high demand in such positions. To have a middle-level manager be competent in critical thinking (as opposed to problem solving in their specialty), one who constantly asks why or should we instead of executing the decisions from on high in an efficient manner, would likely impede the efficient operation of the bureaucracy itself.

RATIONALIZATION OF POLITICS

In an ideal democracy, all citizens share political power equally. Today's nations are too large and complex for direct participation by everyone, which makes elected, representative government the established norm in the industrial West. One of the major difficulties with modern representative democracy is the apathy or indifference of its citizens. There has been a decline in voter turnout for national elections since the 1960s. Today, only about 60 to 70 percent of registered voters actually vote in presidential elections, and voter turnout for state and local elections is much smaller. Because many voters never register, these figures actually overestimate the extent of citizen involvement in the political process. To illustrate, suppose there are 100 eligible voters for a presidential election (n = 100). Of these, 70 percent actually register to vote (n = 70); of these, 70 percent actually go to the voting booth (n = 49); and of these, 70 percent vote for the Democrat (n = 34). The 49 people who actually vote are not a random sample of the population. Studies of voters reveal that people with higher education and income levels are much more likely to participate. Yet, the hypothetical 34 people out of a possible 100 have given the Democratic candidate a huge so-called mandate to rule in the name of the majority of the people. (A mandate is increasingly being defined by political commentators as anything larger than 51 percent of the vote.) The goal of political campaigns is to win the political mandate, that is, to win elections. The goal of the citizen is to influence elected officials to support their interests and values in government legislation and decision making. The relentless pursuit of these goals by candidates and the electorate, often at all costs, has taken us a long way from our civic-book lessons. The ever more efficient steps to achieve these two narrow goals, money to run expensive campaigns and political influence for those outside of government, have overwhelmed all other considerations, including personal ethics, values, and beliefs on the part of politicians and their managers, as well as the broader social values of democracy itself.

Rise of Money

Money has long been central to American politics. Theodore Roosevelt spent $2.5 million on his presidential campaign in 1904, with about three-quarters of the money coming from corporations (Harwood 1997). In 1996, spending on the presidential election reached about $1 billion. The ability to raise large sums of money and run campaigns on the basis of massive television advertising has become the main point of the political campaign. In 1996, estimates are that total spending for all elections in the United States exceeded $3 billion (*The Economist* 1997b), although some place it closer to $4 billion (Harwood 1997). Elections for the House of Representatives and Senate alone were at least $660 million in 1996 (excluding the $30 million that Michael Huffington spent pursuing a California Senate seat in 1994). The average Senate campaign now costs about $4.5 million. In order to pay for their campaigns, it is estimated that senators must raise about $14,000 every week of their six-year term (*The Economist* 1997b). The pursuit of money by politicians to pay for expensive advertising has completely distorted representative democracy.

Groups that have a particular stake in legislation influence legislators and officials of the executive branch. They include physicians, insurance companies, realtors, oil companies, and numerous other groups. Etzioni (1984) defined these as special interest groups because their social base is relatively narrow, entry into the group is restricted, and they are usually concerned about laws and policies that affect their exclusive economic interests. Special interest groups are responsible for a good deal of the obscene amounts of money in political campaigns because they may be focused on such narrow issues as sugar subsidies or oil pricing, which can be worth billions to the members of these special interests.

Although an individual's contribution to a political candidate is limited to $2,000, there are a number of ways that special interest groups can contribute to political campaigns. One way is to set up a Political Action Committee (PAC). There are now about 4,000 PACs, and they contribute about one-third of all campaign money. The vast majority of this money comes from special interests that represent business, professional organizations, or labor (Etzioni 1984; *The Economist* 1997b). PAC money contributed directly to a candidate must be reported to the Federal Elections Commission, and there are limits of $5,000 per candidate (an additional $5,000 can be given in primaries).

There are, however, additional ways to get money to the candidates that interest groups favor. Interest groups encourage the senior management of their member organizations to contribute directly to candidates. The donations from one organization's management team can easily top a PAC donation. Another method is for the interest group to stage fundraisers or receptions for candidates in their home districts, thereby raising money for favored politicians while staying under the legal limits for direct donations. Also, unlimited funds can legally be given by PACs and individuals as "soft money," which is given to political parties for grass-roots party building. These funds often find their way into the campaign coffers of candidates. Still another outlet for unlimited funds is called independent money, for such things as issue advocacy ads. As long as these ads are not formally coordinated with a candidate's campaign, and make no mention of the name of a candidate, they are subject to neither legal limits nor reporting. (These are the ads that end with such statements as "Call Jim Bunning and tell him to stop messing with our social security.")

The money is not spread around to all politicians equally. Special interest groups and their lobbyists focus on key legislators to represent their views. Tom Scully, chief executive officer for the American Federation of Health Systems, is quoted on this point: "There are about 20 major players who decide hospitals' fates. We pick out 10 to 12 that we work with the most and make sure all their local hospital people know them" (Hudson 1996, 5).

As a result of all this money, many critics claim, we have the best Congress that money can buy. Elected representatives argue that the money does not buy votes; it just goes to legislators who happen to believe in the same issues and causes as the special interest group. Although it is true that a quid pro quo relationship cannot be proved, the circumstantial evidence that special interests are buying the votes of our elected officials is substantial. At the very least, the litany of special interest money in our politics demonstrates that the present system encourages the election of officials who represent the interests of powerful organizations. So, taking their claims at face value, what sorts of representation do special interest groups get for their campaign and soft money contributions? And, perhaps more importantly, what sorts of representation do the rest of us receive? For example:

From 1992 through 1994, proenvironment advocates gave $2 million in national political contributions, PACs opposed to environmental regulation gave $24 million (Breslow et al. 1996).

In 1994, the Health Insurance Association of America ran a soft-money advertising campaign directly against President Clinton's health care reform proposal. The "Harry and Louise" advertising blitz was widely credited with undermining support for the president's proposal and with setting the stage for the insurance industry's takeover of health care along similar managed-care lines (albeit corporate-managed instead of government-managed).

Between 1985 and 1995, physicians and the health insurance industry have contributed some $49 million to congressional campaigns and soft-money accounts (Breslow et al. 1996). The focus now is on trying to influence the federal restructuring of Medicare and Medicaid so that physicians, hospitals, insurance companies, and other health care organizations will not be hurt (Hudson 1996; Breslow et al. 1996).

Since the end of the cold war, the B-2 stealth bomber has been a plane without a military mission. Even the Air Force refused to request any more planes, and President Clinton did not include it in his 1997 budget. Northrop Grumman Corporation, along with five subcontractors on the B-2, contributed some $2.2 million to federal candidates in 1993–94. Congress added $493 million to the budget for the bomber (Breslow et al. 1996).

The National Association of Broadcasters, a lobbying group that represents the television industry, contributed more than $800,000 in campaign contributions in the 1996 election. At the same time, the top 75 media markets sold $400 million in political ads in the campaign (Jenkins 1997).

The sugar industry made some $1.8 million in PAC contributions to federal candidates in 1993–94. In return, like-minded congressmen continue price supports that were worth millions to the sugar industry (Breslow et al. 1996).

Rise of Factionalism

Two other types of interest groups combine with special interest groups to present a somewhat different problem for democracy, that of factionalism in government. Single-issue groups come together because of their feelings about specific issues, such as gun control, abortion, or the death penalty. Finally, there are the relatively new phenomena of broad-based organizations, such as the American Association of Retired Persons or Common Cause. Etzioni labeled these groups as constituency-representing organizations, or CROs. They differ from special interest groups in that the social base of CROs is relatively broad, and they often encompass nonmonetary interests (such as values or social status). Although CROs use money to further their ends with the political class, they are not usually in the same money league with special interest groups (although there are some exceptions to this). To be successful, CROs and single interest groups must also be able to motivate their members to contribute small sums of money for their lobbying activity and, most especially, to vote in accordance with the issues of the group. The size of the group, its degree of organization, and the money at its disposal are keys in determining the amount of influence the group has over the political process.

Trying to influence state legislators and members of Congress is the principal activity of all interest groups. Most have professional lobbyists (full- or part-time, depending on the size and power of the group) who try to convince lawmakers to pass legislation that the group desires or to oppose legislation that the group considers to be counter to their interests. One of the tools of lobbyists is to provide information (from the interest group's perspective) to lawmakers on legislative proposals that concern the group. Because government has grown so complex, the information provided by a lobbyist can be crucial in swaying a legislator's vote. In addition, lobbyists cultivate friendships and throw lavish parties in their attempts to influence the legislative process. Promises of political support (or threats of opposition) from interest groups with large memberships can also be effective if the organization can actually deliver its promises and mobilize its members to vote and work for particular candidates. The number of lobbyists and organized interest groups have grown dramatically in recent years.

In 1997, $1.17 billion was spent for lobbying Congress, the White House, and the federal bureaucracy. Some 14,484 lobbyists (outnumbering Representatives by 27 to 1) work on behalf of companies, labor unions, professional associations, and other interest groups. Their goal is to make the interest group's views heard on such issues as managed care (the American Medical Association spent $17.1 million), smoking (tobacco companies spent $15.8 million), telecommunications (the industry spent $63.96 million), pharmaceuticals ($59.7 million), oil and gas ($51.7 million), the automobile industry ($34.6 million), and defense ($40 million) (Salant 1998).

There are two major reasons for the growth in the number and power of interest groups in the United States. First is the growth in the technology of group organization and communications. There has been an explosion of technologies, such as personal computers, fax machines, electronic mail, list-serves, cellular phones, and newsletters since the 1960s. This communications technology has been augmented by the proliferation of digitized information in the form of magazine, charity, and political mailing lists; census data; financial information; and questionnaire data that have been collected by both public and private agencies. The use of this information, along with powerful computer software, allows interest groups to recruit, propagandize, coordinate, and mobilize the actions of their members across the country.

Interest-group generated protests are becoming more efficient and subtler in their techniques. The Christian Coalition, for example, has developed "Hypotenuse," a sophisticated method of generating the needed constituent anger: "Executive director Randy Tate records a request to his membership, usually about the need to pass or defeat legislation. Hypotenuse then sends the audio message, along with a digitized call sheet, via modem to personal computers around the nation. Those PCs, in turn, dial the preselected coalition leaders, deliver Tate's message, and thus spawn a wave of letter writing and phone calling from thousands of people who have already been trained in political action" (Birnbaum 1997, 148). Birnbaum also reported on grass-roots–generating innovations that involve the use of the World Wide Web. One site dedicated to global warming that opposes mandatory cutbacks of greenhouse gasses provides "predrafted E-mails from farmers, senior citizens, and small-business owners that read as if they were self-composed and can be launched directly to congressional representatives with the click of a mouse" (Birnbaum 1997, 149). Whenever Congress or a state legislature threatens the interest of the group, the special interest organization sounds the alarm through its communications network, which brings a flood of phone calls, faxes, letters, and petitions to the offending legislators.

A second reason for the growth in the number of interest groups is the proliferation of government policies and programs that have a direct effect on the well-being of an increasing number of people. Until recently, lobbying was done mainly on the behalf of corporate interests. Now, it has spread to the middle classes as well. Interest groups now include the National Taxpayers' Union, the American Association of Sex Educators, the Possum Growers and Breeders Association, the American Association of Retired Persons, the National Rifle Association, and the Beer Drinkers of America. All of these groups use lobbyists, campaign monies, and votes to influence legislators to allocate government resources according to their interests — most notably in the form of taxbreaks and resisting cuts in favored programs.

Jonathan Rauch (1995) maintained that the proliferation of new interest groups is causing demosclerosis, clogging the arteries of government and preventing it from controlling its own budget, solving new problems, or adapting to economic change. Although CROs and single interest groups are usually not as powerful as the corporate and professional special interests (and, one could argue, they tend to be more representative in their make-up), all of them combined have a paralyzing effect on government. Propose a national health policy and the medical insurance industry pays for a fatal multimedia campaign. Propose an energy tax to encourage conservation and reduce the deficit, and the oil industry fights you tooth and nail. Suggest cutting the business lunch deduction from 80 percent to 50 percent and the National Restaurant Association will mobilize to kill it. A *Time* cover story on "hyper democracy" summed up the irrationality factor of interest group politics: "It means that the corruption of the public interest by special interests is no easily cured pathology, but a stubbornly rational pattern of behavior. The costs of each groups' selfishness are spread across the whole nation while the benefits are captured by the group. Though every group might prosper in the long run if all groups surrendered just enough to balance the budget, it makes no sense for any of them to surrender unilaterally" (Wright 1995, 5). The rationalization of politics as exhibited by the proliferation of interest groups is counter to the national interest. Rational action in pursuit of the narrow goals of the organization often leads an organization to undermine the very foundations of the system.

So, it would seem that the rationalization of politics runs counter to the interests of the entire political system. Interest groups and their money undermine the geographical basis for representative government and substitute representation of moneyed interests in its place. This is no small matter. In a democracy, everyone is supposed to have equal access to the ear of government, but to quote the pigs in *Animal Farm* "some are more equal than others." Who does a congressman from western Kentucky represent on the floor of the House when he gets hundreds of thousands of dollars from the Savings and Loan industry to run for the seat in his district? How is a Senator to reconcile any conflicts between the interests of her constituents and the interests of the National Education Association when she relies on its money and volunteers to win her next election? Our elected officials in Washington and at the state level are trapped in a system in which they must be perpetually on the make for campaign contributions. They are in chronic need of campaign cash for their next election, cash that will be given (at least on a continuing basis) only in return for their support. And the problem is systemic. As in any crisis that results from the irrationality factor, one cannot unilaterally forego the money or special interest support and expect to win elections.

The tie between a representative and an interest group is far more pervasive and arguably stronger than the tie between a representative and the voters back home. In classical democratic theory, representatives have to face the voters only on a periodic basis; in actual practice, they must continuously mine the pockets of interest groups. However, even this tenuous tie between politician and voter, in which the politician must garner support for his policies from his constituencies, has been rationalized as well.

Rise of the Managers

Concurrent with the rise of big money in the political process, a new breed of campaign managers and consultants has emerged. Their lack of restraint is readily apparent from the title of the books they write. *Bare Knuckles and Back Rooms: My Life in American Politics* by Ed Rollins and Tom Defrank (1996); or *All's Fair: Love, War, and Running for President* by James Carville, Mary Matalin, and Peter Knobler (1994). An exception would be *Behind the Oval Office: Winning the Presidency in the Nineties* by Dick Morris (1997), which perhaps reflects Morris's penchant for deception and manipulation rather than outright war. Books and articles written about these hired guns also zero in on the theme of lack of restraint. Titles include *Bad Boy: The Life and Politics of Lee Atwater* (Brady 1996); *Whatever It Takes: The Real Struggle for Political Power in America* (Drew 1997); *War Without Bloodshed: The Art of Politics* (Clift & Brazaitis 1997); *Manipulating the Candidate* (Rust 1997); and my personal favorite, *The "Conniving Worm" Factor* (Levine 1997). That they represent something beyond the constraints of traditional American politics there should be no doubt.

There are about 7,000 full-time professionals in the campaign consultant field (Levine 1997), though some estimates are as high as 30,000 if part-time consultants and those who emerge every election year are added (Rust 1997). Billings by consultants were estimated to be about $1 billion in the 1996 elections (Levine 1997). They have their own professional association, the American Association of Political Consultants, and their own journal, *Campaigns and Elections*, with a circulation of about 70,000 (Rust 1997).

Although few boys and girls want to grow up to be political consultants, this too may be changing. Michael Rust (1997) reported that a number of graduate programs have predictably (in terms of the rationalization of higher education) been started in political management. In line with recent practitioners, one can well imagine that such programs will push the limits of objectivity to encourage the profession to work for anyone with the money to pay them, much like the ideology of defense lawyers who defend anyone, or scientists who will work on weapons of mass destruction. Salaries in the field of political management are comparable with public relations jobs at the same level — at the Washington level, salaries start around $60,000.

The vast numbers of consultants work at the state and local level, but the real stars work in national campaigns. Political consultants and managers are needed by candidates to raise money, organize advertising, arrange travel, schedule events, and hire and manage staff. They also contract with advertising producers, coordinate with other groups (such as the party), conduct polls (so that the candidate knows which bold positions to take), and devise winning campaign strategies. Rust, however, summed up their basic job in one word: manipulation.

Advances in the techniques of manipulation have come from the social sciences as well as advertising. Campaign operatives — many of whom have no discernable political beliefs except winning elections — manipulate the press through photo opportunities, and "spin doctors." Focus groups and survey information can uncover the emotional levers that will get us to buy a deodorant or a candidate. Advertising through mass media can pull many of these levers at will. Campaign organizations can target their propaganda by obtaining mailing lists from magazines, special interest organizations, organizational and professional rolls, and the Federal Elections Commission of people who are likely to respond to the message. Major corporations use the same or similar lists to market their goods and services more efficiently.

In classical democratic theory, elections are intended to hold politicians accountable to the people; the vote is an exercise of sovereign power. Elections today could just as easily be thought of as contests between two candidates over market shares (in fact, elections today are thought of explicitly in these terms by the hired political operatives who dominate the election process). The same advertising agencies that sell us Pepsi

Cola and Secret deodorant also pitch candidates to us in local and national elections, and the advertising techniques are the same. The techniques rely on the manipulation of symbols in an attempt to create a bridge between a consumer's unconscious desires, fears, or anxieties and the product being sold. The objective is to get consumers to believe that the purchase of the product will make their dreams come true or that they will be able to avoid their worst fears. Similarly, effective campaigners try to project a positive image and connect it to flag, family values, or military strength.

Consultant Dick Morris, who is infamous for moving back and forth between parties as a political hired gun (as well as being infamous for other things), is clearly focused on image over substance. By consulting polls in order to put the best public face on his candidate, he even designed the president's vacations: Martha's Vineyard, he believed, was too elitist; instead Clinton should hike with high-tech gear because hikers and technology lovers were swing-voters. As a rule, according to Morris, the president went along, but when Morris suggested that the president should stop playing golf ("a Dole-voter activity") Clinton declined (and many say this president stands for nothing!).

Alternatively, negative campaigning, which appears to be more prevalent today, attempts to smear opponents with half-truths and innuendo and connect their image with special interests (defined as the other candidate's PACs), licentiousness, or greed. Here is a report on one "Pollie" award-winning attack ad on Rep. Bill Baker (CA) at the 1997 American Association of Political Consultants meeting produced by media consultant Joe White: White's ad opened with an ominous voice reading words that flashed on the screen accompanied by shots of an evil-looking Baker. "Baseball players who spit in an umpire's face. Politicians who shut down the government to get even." The spot ended by showing Baker wading into a crowd to "attack" a protester at a political rally. "Don't we deserve better?" (Levine 1997, 2). Finally, there are the new, rapid response ads that run to counter the negative advertising of opponents. Here is a report on the extensive research and development by President Clinton's campaign committee for responding quickly and efficiently to expected Dole attack ads:

Beginning in January, Squier, Knapp and Sheinkopf produced the kind of attack spots they expected from Dole. Penn and Schoen would test the in-house negative ads, then help come up with better ads to rebut them. Sheinkopf, a connoisseur of campaign hardball, hatched the ugliest attacks he could think of. Penczner then used an advertising technique called animatics, video rough cuts using

> dummy images that could be transmitted by computer to the malls where Penn and Schoen were testing the ads. Penczner and Knapp's people created a library of B-roll images, scowling Dole/Gingrich couplings, laughing children, kindly senior, forceful Clinton — any of which could be popped into the animatic to create a spot quickly and cheaply. Clinton's response ads were tested, refined and retested until they actually left voters feeling better about the President than they had before seeing the original Dole attack. (Stengel & Pooley 1996, 12).

Campaigns and political rhetoric have little to do with issues beyond the level of bumper-sticker slogans. Although these techniques are effective in winning elections (as they are in selling deodorant) they are harmful to the political system as a whole. Democracy can survive only if people make rational choices on the basis of enlightened self-interest of the variety described by Alexis de Tocqueville and Durkheim. In a 30-second television spot there is little time for serious consideration of political issues.

Although what could be termed the corruption of the political campaign is widely recognized, it is usually perceived as a slight problem in democratic procedures, one in need of reform but certainly nothing that threatens the foundations of the system. After all, it is reasoned, trivial, issue-less campaigns are well known in American history. Such a view ignores the present-day sophistication and pervasiveness of manipulative technology and techniques and ignores the billions of dollars needed to run these campaigns.

CONCLUSION

The title of this chapter is an image from Yeats's poem "The Second Coming." It is an image of disintegration. The gyre is the special pattern that the falcon flies when it is released from the falconer. Looking for prey, the bird flies up and out in ever widening circular patterns. What holds the falcon to the falconer? The falcon is a wild, natural animal. It has been captured, tamed, trained, and cared for lovingly. The bond between falcon and falconer is built on nature. The freedom of the trained falcon is real not withstanding that it is bound to the falconer by an invisible tie. The bird has been trained to return even when it has been set free. The falcon obeys; all are served.

And yet, when we watch a falcon after its release, we wonder if, this time, it will not come back. How wide the gyre before the tether — the invisible tether — breaks? Will the falcon's widening freedom break the civilized bond?

The forces that truly constitute any civilization worth preserving (or worth worrying about its disintegration) are invisible. They are like the bond between a falcon and a falconer. Yeats saw that the power of a society is precisely its gift of granting and ordering (governing) freedom in the same gesture. The social bond consists of tradition, ethical and religious values, enlightened self-interest, and love and commitment. The social bond is necessary for individual freedom and social order to coexist. These bonds are loosening — a loosening that imperils us all.

8

New Ideology

There is a very different view of advanced industrial society, one that is almost diametrically opposed to the view presented in these pages, which is vaguely labeled as postindustrialism. This perspective holds that contemporary American society is in the midst of a profound transformation from an industrial infrastructure to one that is based on new technologies and resources. Alvin Toeffler likened it to a "third wave" of infrastructural change (the other two waves were the agrarian and industrial revolutions) that will dramatically transform our sociocultural systems. The increasing adoption of new technologies, postindustrialists assert, is changing our social relationships by leveling the great disparities of wealth and power and making them available to all. The transition from an industrial to postindustrial society is ushering in a new era in which our values of equality, democracy, and human affection for one another will blossom. All we need to do, many of the postindustrialists claim, is continue with technological intensification and utopia will be achieved. In this chapter I examine these claims and the evidence on which they are based.

POSTINDUSTRIALISM

The term "postindustrialism," originally coined by Daniel Bell, is now generally used to refer to a future society that is based on a qualitatively different mode of production that has been variously described as based on service, information, or biological technology. Although postindustrialists are in some disagreement over the foundations of the postindustrial system, they are in apparent agreement that this new mode of production will greatly extend the environmental limits of depletion and pollution. This extension will come about through more efficient technology (biotechnology or computer communications, for example) or the widespread adoption of new social practices (the change from manufacturing to the production of services) that are less hostile to the environment. Postindustrialists rarely address the degradation of the environment directly; they seem merely to assume that these problems will be solved so that they can get on with the more serious business of forecasting the future.

Consistent with the technological world view, prophets of postindustrialism see technology as the solution to all our problems. According to this view, many of the ills that have vexed society from the beginning of civilization will be eliminated with the adoption of new technologies. Bill Gates exemplifies this optimism:

> It should be obvious by now that I'm an optimist about the impact of the new technology. It will enhance our leisure time and enrich our culture by expanding the distribution of information. It will help relieve pressures on urban areas by enabling people to work from home or remote-site offices. It will relieve pressures on natural resources because increasing numbers of products will take the form of bits rather than manufactured goods. It will give us more control over our lives, enabling us to tailor our experiences and the products we use to our interest. Citizens of the information society will enjoy new opportunities for productivity, learning, and entertainment. (Gates 1997, 284)

For Gates, the coming information age, advanced by computers and the information superhighway, will transform our life much as the industrial revolution transformed agrarian societies.

Gates identified efficiency and resulting productivity as the engine of sociocultural change. "Productivity is the engine that drives improvements in any system. When we want better medical practice, we find ways to deliver treatment less expensively or more effectively or both. When we want cheaper food, we find ways to make agriculture more efficient. . . . If we want better education — faster learning and better understanding — we have to find ways to get greater results for every dollar we spend" (Gates 1997, 214). This drive for efficiency through human organization and the development of new technologies, postindustrialists argue, is fundamentally changing industrial societies.

Postindustrialists see the possibility (some see the inevitability) of the new technologies becoming the foundation for a whole new social order. John Naisbitt, author of *Megatrends* (1982), for example, believes that information itself will become the new form of wealth. Naisbitt points out that since the 1950s, information occupations, defined as clerks and professionals, have increased from about 17 percent of the workforce to more than 60 percent today. This is the result, he argues, of a shift in the strategic resources of American society. In an industrial society, the key resource is capital; that is, capital can be used to create wealth. In an information society the key resource is information; it is knowledge that creates value and wealth. Because information can flow so freely through computer networks and can be acquired by almost anyone, information will not cause the kinds of stratification associated with traditional forms of property.

Postindustrialists have noted a shift in the occupational structure of modern society. In the decades after World War II, the United States dominated the world economy. In 1960, Naisbitt reported that the United States produced about 25 percent of the world's manufactured goods. Today, the United States produces less than 17 percent. Japan, Naisbitt claimed (somewhat prematurely it would now seem), would become the world's leading industrial power. It is simply too late, he noted, for the United States to recapture the industrial lead. Other countries in the Third World, with their supplies of cheap labor (and no labor unions) and abundant resources (and lack of environmental protection), are much better equipped to provide high-quality manufactured goods. Furthermore, in the new world economy, all countries are increasingly interdependent. As the Third World takes over major industrial tasks, the developed countries must "move beyond the industrial past, towards the great new enterprises of the future" (Naisbitt 1982, 58). These industries include electronics, biotechnology, robotics, alternative energy sources, and seabed mining.

Postindustrialists forecast the elimination of most boring jobs; the "electronic cottage" where much of our work can be done at home; increased leisure time; a more highly educated workforce; and increased opportunities for personal creativity. Robots will replace any remaining manufacturing jobs in the developed nations and most of the population will work in service industries, management (and management consulting), and high-tech industries.

Gates carries this vision even further. He forecasts a time when computers and new forms of communication will also make outmoded many middle-level managerial positions, as well as extend the productivity of professionals through the development of computerized "expert systems" and the flow of information on the information highway. Although the elimination of many jobs will be painful, Gates maintains, new occupations will rise (most of which we do not even know of yet) to replace the old foundations of the middle classes. This is why Gates is also a great believer in investing in a productive educational system, one made more efficient through computers and the information superhighway, to help people retool for these new, unknown positions of the future.

Decentralization

Naisbitt also forecasted a time of decentralization, as political and economic decisions are increasingly handled at local levels. The federal government, Naisbitt claimed, is largely becoming obsolete; state and local governments are fast becoming the most important political powers in the United States. The centralization of political power in the United States, Naisbitt argued, paralleled the industrialization process. Industrialism required enormous centralization to coordinate labor, raw materials, and capital. The Great Depression ushered in an increased role for government in the econ-omy and the two world wars and need for full mobilization also caused centralized governments to grow. However, Naisbitt argued, conditions change. With the decline in manufacturing, decentralization has now become the new organizational form in the United States.

The bulk of Naisbitt's decentralization argument rests on the decline in the power of the federal government and the consequent rise in powers of state and local governments. Real power, Naisbitt asserted, has shifted away from the legislative and executive branches of the federal government to the states, cities, towns, and neighborhoods. Congress has become largely obsolete; since President Reagan's administration, power has been transferred from Washington to local governments. States are becoming increasingly active in such areas as fighting organized crime, environmental protection, and building mass transit systems. In addition, states are beginning to band together to further their mutual interests. Naisbitt was hard pressed to cite any data to indicate that big business in America is getting smaller (data that cite the exact opposite were presented in Chapter 3 of this book). Instead, he asserted, businesses have decentralized their operations. More and more, corporations are locating major plants in rural areas. Decisions in these plants are often left to local managers and, increasingly, in the hands of people who are directly affected by organizational decisions.

Postindustrialists also forecast the crumbling of bureaucratic hierarchies, which will be replaced by informal networks of people who work together in loose associations, sharing information and resources. There are several factors responsible for the decline of hierarchical organizations, according to Naisbitt. First, bureaucracies have proven to be inflexible in the new information society. They tend to slow down the flow of information, just as greater speed and flexibility become needed. Second, we will move toward networking in response to Japanese competition. Workers in Japan, Naisbitt reported, meet in small, decentralized work groups and people at the top listen to their decisions (apparently that these are mandatory meetings, on the workers own time, was not widely known when Naisbitt wrote his book). Third, people are becoming increasingly dissatisfied with the impersonal nature of bureaucratic institutions. With the decline of primary groups in our society, such as the extended family, community, and church, people need to feel involved in their work. The typical bureaucratic hierarchy prevents this sort of identification. Fourth and finally, younger, more educated workers are filling up the workplace. More than 40 percent of the baby boom generation has a college education; there is simply not enough room for all this college talent at the top. For all these reasons, Naisbitt claimed, networks, not bureaucracies, are the wave of the future. Gates seconded this decentralization argument with his focus on the information superhighway. He made numerous observations on the elimination of middlemen; extending the productivity of professionals; and praising the flexibility of small, lean, efficient companies that will fiercely compete through product innovation and price on an international scale.

Participatory Democracy

Because of this decentralization of institutions, many postindustrialists argue, participatory democracy will flower. Technology will allow people to vote directly on issues that concern them. According to Naisbitt, citizens, workers, and consumers are demanding and receiving a greater voice in the affairs of government and the corporations. The 1970s marked the beginning of the participatory era of political life, as indicated by the growth in the use of referenda and initiatives. This, wrote Naisbitt, marked a gradual shift in power away from elected representatives and appointed officials to the people themselves. Although Naisbitt did not predict the demise of representative democracy, he did predict that more of the serious issues that people care about will be dealt with directly by voters through referenda and initiatives. Politicians, some of whom are directly influenced by these dreams (Gary Hart, Ross Perot, and Newt Gingrich, for example) have taken up this call, proposing such things as town meetings and computer referenda on legislation and trade agreements. Gates was much less enthusiastic about direct democracy in his book. He believes there is a place for representatives — middlemen that add value to the political process — but he does see an interactive network that allows political debate and dialogue to be far more efficient, easier to organize, and, therefore, far more effective in influencing representatives through lobbying and referendums (Gates 1997, 308).

The demand for direct participation also extends to the economic areas of our lives. According to Naisbitt, consumerism is alive and well in the latter half of the twentieth century. Consumers appear less militant only because they have stopped pressing for more government regulation. The new push will be toward direct representation on corporate boards. Groups other than the affluent, such as workers, community leaders, and activist shareholders, will increasingly gain a voice in the running of corporate America.

Gates did not directly echo this position (perhaps for obvious reasons), but he seconds the overall vision of economic democracy with his version of a "friction free capitalism." Gates posited that advances in computers and communications force capitalism to move closer to the ideal of the perfect market. "When Adam Smith described the concept of markets in *Wealth of Nations* in 1776, he theorized that if every buyer knew every seller's price and every seller knew what every buyer was willing to pay, everyone in the 'market' would be able to make fully informed decisions and society's resources would be distributed efficiently" (Gates 1997, 181). Through a broad-band, global, interactive network, producers will have the information to gauge what buyers want much more efficiently, and consumers will have the information to buy more efficiently. Of necessity, this would keep providers of goods and services far more attuned to the needs of the marketplace.

A final trend toward participatory democracy detailed by Naisbitt is workers' rights. The baby boom generation (people born from 1946 to 1963) has invaded the workplace with its "alien" values of individualism, high level of education, and rebellious attitude toward authority. Through sheer force of numbers they are forcing corporations to recognize the rights of employees, including free speech, privacy, and due process in employee firing. Increasingly, Naisbitt argued, the trend in postindustrial societies is toward the involvement of people whose lives are affected in the decision-making process. Gates seconded this opinion by writing of the need to involve workers in the success of the company — often through stock options. Such activities, he posited, will allow even large companies to more efficiently create innovative products and services and keep quality high and costs low for the benefit of the global market and the benefit of all societies.

All of this glorious technological paradise will be achieved, most postindustrialists argue, only if we sit back and allow technological development to run its course. Rarely do postindustrialists directly address the problems caused by this new technology. Gates is a major exception. He wrote of many critical issues — potential problems caused by the widespread adoption of new technologies. Like many postindustrialists, he has a pronounced faith that technological solutions will be developed to deal with these problems, but almost alone among postindustrialists, Gates occasionally advocates direct social action to ameliorate some of the worst problems associated with new technologies. The others, it would seem, advocate that new technology should evolve with little human intervention — with faith that the resulting changes in the sociocultural system will be of tremendous benefit to all.

WEAKNESS OF POSTINDUSTRIALISM

The weakness of postindustrialism is readily apparent in the predictions postindustrialists make about the occupational structure of their new society. They forecast a society based on the production of information and services. This future is projected on the basis of several trends. The growth of the service economy in the 1950s was the first change of the occupational structure noted by postindustrialists. In that decade, the number of service jobs in the American economy had actually overtaken the number of manufacturing jobs. Since that time, the service sector has remained the dominant sector of employment.

What futurists fail to note, however, is that the growth in service occupations has been a part of the industrialization process from the beginning. Service jobs have been growing at a faster rate than manufacturing jobs in the United States since the 1860s (Kumar 1978). The growth of services in industrial society is related to the decline of the extended family and community as a provider of such services as childcare, counseling, and social security. As industrialization continues to intensify, demands for geographic and social mobility will continue to weaken the community, as well as the extended family and, as has been seen more recently, the nuclear family, thus putting even more demand on the service industries. Services that used to be performed by virtue of family or personal ties, such as preparing meals and helping the sick and the elderly, are increasingly being performed by government or being integrated into the market economy. Not realizing that the growth of the service sector is an integral part of industrialization itself, many futurists seized upon the trend, extrapolated it into the future, and forecasted a society based on service industries. Calling forth images of a society based on the provision of services, futurists failed to recognize the continuity of the present with the past. Identifying what they took to be a new trend, they extrapolated that trend into the future without any regard for system limits. Almost as bad, they misidentified the trend itself.

The tendency for futurists who write of the growing service economy is to focus on those services that are professional in character. They call forth images of lawyers and doctors and managerial consultants. However, the actual growth in the service sector has been quite different. Unfortunately, the service occupations on the rise are the relatively low-pay, low-skill, low-prestige service jobs — fast-food workers, kitchen helpers, sales clerks, custodians, and nurses' aides and orderlies. These jobs are precisely the unskilled occupations one would expect if government and the market economy were providing services to fill the void left by the decline in family and community.

A similar misunderstanding has occurred with the second occupational trend that has been recognized by many futurists, the growth in high-tech information occupations. Postindustrialists call forth images of computer scientists, programmers, and data processors, but the reality is far different. Jobs that dominate the information sector are the traditional grunt jobs associated with bureaucracy — secretaries, clerks, and typists (though now, equipped with personal computers). These are the very jobs one would expect to predominate as industrialism becomes more intensive and bureaucracies grow in power and scope to provide the necessary coordination. The growth of bureaucracy has had a close association with industrialization from the beginning.

The postindustrialists are correct in asserting that advanced industrial economies are rapidly undergoing a transition in employment from the production of manufactured goods to the production of services and information, but this shift is of the employment of human beings in the production process, not a decline in the industrial mode of production itself. In fact, the shift is consistent with the intensification of industrialism. The purpose of a mode of production is to draw energy and raw materials out of the environment and convert them to human use. Recent developments, such as increasing global competition, an increasingly depleted environment, and some worker safety and pollution abatement mandates, have threatened the profit margins of many industrial companies. As Marx and others pointed out years ago, in order to maintain or increase profit margins, companies attempt to minimize what they pay their employees. Domestic capital flows overseas in search of cheaper labor (and no labor unions, environmental controls, or worker safety mandates). Manufacturing jobs that remain are becoming increasingly automated. The whole point of technology is to apply it to traditional agriculture, mining, office work, the provision of services, and manufacturing to make them more productive and, thus, more profitable. The impact of the application of technology in these areas has always been to reduce the number of workers needed.

The manufacturing jobs being lost are among the highest-paid working-class occupations. For the working classes, these jobs are being rapidly replaced by jobs in the service and information sectors — jobs that require minimal skills and education and that offer little prestige, personal satisfaction, autonomy, or income. Nor can the production jobs in high technology (or sunrise industries as postindustrialists often call them) replace the loss of traditional manufacturing jobs. New high-tech manufacturing jobs generally do not pay as well as manufacturing jobs in traditional industries (particularly jobs in the old-line oligopolies). The high-tech industry is fiercely competitive (at least at this writing). The new jobs are also subject to the same forces of automation and cheaper foreign labor as the traditional manufacturing jobs.

The prediction that high technology and the production of services and information will become the foundation of a postindustrial system appears to stem from a serious misunderstanding of the function of the mode of production. A mode of production can be defined as technologies and social practices that are employed for extracting energy and raw materials from the environment and fashioning them for human use. Industrialism is a process; it is constantly employing science and new technologies in its quest to more efficiently exploit the natural environment. Again, the postindustrialists miss the point of new technologies. New technologies are not ends in themselves; they are a means to increase productivity. Society cannot live by high-tech alone; we cannot eat computer chips. Nor can we have an infrastructure based only on the provision of services and information. "Even the highest-tech office is built with steel and cement, pipes and wires. People working in services will buy all sorts of things — more software, sure, but also more sport utility vehicles. As the Department of Energy economist Arthur Rypinsi says, 'The information age has arrived, but even so people still get hot in the summer and cold in the winter. And even in the information age it tends to get dark at night'" (McKibben 1998, 77). The rapid growth of services has been an integral part of industrialization from the beginning; it is folly to extrapolate from this trend without its industrial base. We cannot all live by selling each other hamburgers, insurance, or managerial services.

Power and Control

Postindustrial dreams are founded on an unrealistic faith in high technology and a serious misrepresentation of the impact that high technology is likely to have on our lives. There is little evidence for the assertion that the information society is bringing about a decentralization of power and control. Langdon Winner noted that far from serving to decentralize power in an industrial society, computer and telecommunications technology appear to aid bureaucratization. The primary beneficiaries of the use of large amounts of digitized information, Winner pointed out, are large corporations and public bureaucracies. As international competition for markets and resources becomes more intense, we can expect corporations increasingly to employ new electronics media to become larger as well as more efficient and productive. Public and private bureaucracies will become larger, more complex, and more reliant on computer technology to tighten the coordination of diverse activities. "Current developments in the information age suggest an increase in power by those who already have a great deal of power, an enhanced centralization of control by those already prepared for control and an augmentation of wealth by the already wealthy" (Winner 1984). Telecommunications and computers will further centralize the power within bureaucracies. It is the large-scale organization that has the capital and expertise to collect and manipulate the data; it is the large-scale organization that determines what information is collected and who has access to it.

Evidence of recent government growth cited in Chapter 3 indicates that growth is still going strong. Evidence of a dramatic drop in number of employees, taxes, spending, and power has not been overwhelming. What Naisbitt and other postindustrialists may have picked up on in their decentralization arguments is perhaps better termed a process of disintegration, that is, states and regions asserting their own unique character and interests as opposed to the interests of the larger nation-state.

Although many postindustrialists assert that the widespread availability of personal computers will equalize the relationship between individuals and large organizations, their widespread adoption would not fundamentally change the balance of power. David Burnham picked up on the basic inequality between the individual and large bureaucratic organizations, even when both are equipped with a computer. "Is it reasonable to believe that a dedicated band of environmentalists, sending electronic smoke signals to each other via their home terminals, really will be able to effectively match the concentrated power of a giant oil company or committed government agency?" (Burnham 1980, 14). Beliefs that postindustrialism will usher in a new age of decentralization appear to be based on little more than dreams. Contrary to the expectations of postindustrialists, future society is likely to continue to be dominated by powerful bureaucracies. Though these bureaucracies may be leaner in numbers of workers, they will be far more efficient in attaining their goals.

In order to increase the efficiency of their operations, bureaucracies have harnessed the computer. C. Wright Mills saw the machine for what it is from the start: "Yet we are still only in the beginning of the office-machine age. Only when the machinery and the social organization of the office are fully integrated in terms of maximum efficiency per dollar spent will that age be full blown" (Mills 1951, 195). Bureaucratic efficiency, by definition, lies in hierarchical organization. Accordingly, new technology has been conceived and implemented primarily as an instrument to increase employee efficiency and extend managerial control. Computers have made it possible to eliminate many middle-level management positions, thereby tightening the control of the hierarchy. In manufacturing, computer systems have been designed to coordinate the flow of raw materials, machine time, labor, and other resources. With such systems in place, as we saw in Chapter 4 in the example of the 7-Eleven stores in Japan, the front office can continuously monitor the work environment by making decisions about inventory, manpower, and maintenance needs on a rationalized basis. These same systems of monitoring and control are increasingly being applied to social service agencies and clerical work within government bureaus and corporate organizations. Although local managers will retain some control over those decisions that can be made efficiently on-site (and efficiency and productivity are the point here, not other values such as freedom or autonomy), the use of high-tech computer and communications equipment will only serve to strengthen the structure of authority.

Challenges of Participatory Democracy

One of the chief reasons cited by postindustrialists for the coming participatory democracy in government and the work place is that of the high education and skill levels required in postindustrial occupations. Although postindustrialists have been telling us that the information society will require a more skilled and educated workforce, high technology itself is having a very different effect. The application of computer technology to traditional industrial and service pursuits will not require a highly educated workforce. High technology will lower the overall skill level of the workforce, not raise it (Menosky 1984). Technology appears to follow a skills curve. When new technology is first applied to a job, the skills required to perform that job tend to rise. Initially, job performance requires mastery of old skills (for secretaries that means typing, spelling, punctuation, and grammar) as well as mastery of new skills (the use of complicated word-processing machines and programs). But then, as increasingly sophisticated technology is applied to the job, the technology becomes easier to use and more efficient and comprehensive for performing tasks (spelling, grammar, filing, and so on). One need only think of the computer sophistication of the majority of computer users today compared with ten years ago — the machines and software are increasingly user-friendly and more powerful. The computer revolution has been a revolution of users, not of computer jocks. The skills of the majority of users today are minimal, yet they can perform tasks that would have taxed computer experts just a decade ago. The application of high technology to traditional occupations tends to de-skill those occupations.

Some futurists recognize that low-skilled service and information occupations comprise the bulk of the new jobs being created in contemporary society. However, they point to a trend that many of these jobs are being upgraded in status and responsibilities as high technologies are applied to the job. Krishan Kumar, however, labeled the data to back up this trend as "sociological sleight of hand." By relying on the official statistics of the occupational census, postindustrialists have failed "to ask what real degree of professional expertise, technical training, or education might be involved in the increasingly common practice of assigning 'professional' or 'technical' status to a diverse range of occupations" (Kumar 1978, 214–215). Kumar found that changing a job title suits an employee because it allows the employee to gain more status, and suits an employer because it is good for labor relations — there was little change in the substance of work itself, however.

The rise of the service economy has seen some increase in the semi-professions, such as nursing, social work, medical technology, and teaching, but these professions do not enjoy the prestige, autonomy, or salaries of the traditional professions. Even the traditional professions are becoming highly specialized and increasingly are employed by government or corporate bureaucracies, hierarchical organizations that tend to undermine the autonomy of professionals and routinize their performance (as we saw in Chapter 6 with physicians and other professionals, such as lawyers and scientists). This trend of increasingly subjecting a professional's judgment to the rules and procedures of the organization undercuts the postindustrial claim of freedom and democracy on the job.

Another trend undercutting workplace democracy is the division of labor. The increasing division of labor is the hallmark of an industrial society. It breaks down tasks into ever more routinized tasks. Mills described the process:

> Since the 'twenties it has increased the division of white-collar labor, recomposed personnel, and lowered skill levels. Routine operations in minutely subdivided organizations have replaced the bustling interest of work in well-known groups. Even on managerial and professional levels, the growth of rational bureaucracies has made work more like factory production. The managerial demiurge is constantly furthering all these trends: mechanization, more minute division of labor, the use of less skilled and less expensive workers. (Mills 1951, 226–227)

The "managerial demiurge" that Mills wrote of is his reference to the bureaucratic thrust for coordination and control in order to more efficiently attain the goals of an organization. The ever more minute division of labor, reducing human decision making on the job — thus, mechanizing and standardizing job performance — is one of the chief tools of management while computer and telecommunications allow for increased coordination and control. This increasing division of labor does not prepare men and women well for democracy in the workplace. On the contrary, by limiting their skills, control, and freedom on the job, it prepares them for a much more familiar form of workplace governance.

Nor is participatory democracy on the job or in the general society likely to stem simply from the spread of higher education. The majority of skilled technical and professional jobs in modern society do not require a highly knowledgeable workforce in the traditional sense. Education to attain these jobs has become narrow and focused on technical competence as opposed to educating the whole person. Although there is a traditional liberal arts core left at most universities, it has been pared down to a bare minimum, and what remains has been trivialized. Our best students still exhibit the excitement of discovery, but, more typically, students look at the liberal arts and humanities as something they have to get through in order to attain their desired job credentials — seeing it as an empty academic exercise unconnected to the real world. As I stated in Chapter 7, it is far more likely that our higher-education institutions are producing the type of graduates needed in an advanced bureaucratic industrial society. The need is for specialists and technicians who will pursue the goals of the organization in an efficient manner. The bulk of the jobs in a bureaucratic-industrial society do not require people with critical thinking skills. In fact, such people may hinder the efficient operation of bureaucracies.

It also seems doubtful that the spread of information or personal computers will promote participatory democracy in the larger society. The introduction of television did little to enhance the level of debate in industrial democracies; in fact, it has demonstrably contributed to growing voter apathy and manipulation. Why should computers and telecommunications be any different? Postindustrialists tell us that two-way, interactive telecommunications systems will allow ordinary citizens to participate in the political decision process, but it could just as well have the opposite effect: Widespread adoption of computer and information technology could seriously weaken our traditional rights as well as erode democratic government. The computer aids in the process of centralization by placing more power in the hands of nonelected officials in both public and private bureaucracies.

One trend almost completely ignored by postindustrialists in this regard is the growth in the technology of surveillance and manipulation. The use of sophisticated electronic monitoring systems is pervasive, even in supposedly democratic societies. Governments and private bureaucracies now have access to computer information systems that have the capability of monitoring most of our actions. Credit reports are instantly available to financial institutions, government agencies, and retail outlets. "Social transactions leave digitized footprints that afford opportunities that have a menacing aspect" (Winner 1984, 95). Corporations and governments are quickly eroding our sense of privacy and replacing it with the pervasive feeling of being watched.

The wedding of these sophisticated monitoring devices to computerized information storage and retrieval systems is a civil libertarian's nightmare. Both public and private bureaucracies have grown in their ability to collect, analyze, and distribute large quantities of digitized information. The new tools of the information age are employed by old-line bureaucracies to further enhance their power and thereby, their efficiency. Private and public bureaucracies construct databases that contain information about our financial transactions, criminal records, taxes, credit, magazine subscriptions, employment histories, welfare assistance, health, banking, and other personal data. As a result, we have lost much of our privacy and opened ourselves to manipulation and control by these powerful organizations.

Although Burnham wrote about the abuses of these data systems (such as auditing the taxes of President Nixon's political opponents and the National Security Agency and other intelligence agencies tracking civil rights and antiwar demonstrators), it is the legitimate uses of these databases that are far more frightening. Criminal records are routinely scrutinized, not only by agencies of the criminal justice system but by private corporations seeking information about their employees. Burnham described in detail how computer programs have been used to match the information in many databases. The Department of Health, Education, and Welfare matched the computerized files of federal employees to welfare recipients in order to detect fraud. Selective Service registration and student loans are now routinely matched; those failing to register are denied student loans. Tax rolls and other databases are now routinely used to track down runaway parents and deny tax refunds, at first for those whose children have had to rely on public assistance to live, later for all those who avoided their child-support obligations.

The number and size of these vast databases are growing as bureaucracies seek to increase their power and efficiency. For example, the Federal Reserve Board is encouraging the establishment of electronic fund transfer systems. Designed to streamline banking, the systems will also allow increased electronic monitoring of an individual's financial transactions and status. Another example is the experiments by marketers who have systems that can correlate the buying habits of families with the advertising they view. In Pittsfield, Massachusetts, some 2,000 families were participants in "Behaviorscan." The families received test commercials on their home television sets and the system kept track of every item the family purchased at their local supermarkets. This information was fed into computers that correlated the commercial ads with the family's purchases, thereby determining the most effective ads and enabling advertisers to reach the rest of the population more effectively (Burnham 1980). The use of focus groups and opinion polls to market products and political candidates uncovers similar levers and appeals that will motivate people to engage in a desired action.

The problem with these instruments of efficiency is that they enhance the power over our lives of already powerful organizations. There is little difference between using computer and telecommunications technology to achieve efficient political administration and political manipulation; little difference between their use in efficient marketing and manipulating the marketplace. Virtually unchecked by law or custom, they are the primary tools by which public and private bureaucracies increasingly dominate social, economic, and political life.

Although a two-way, interactive system between the masses and our political (and economic) leaders is still in its infancy, the current popularity of instant public opinion polls gives some indication of how such a system may affect the political process. The use of polling data by politicians is to inform them which stand they can safely take (is the district pro-life or pro-choice?), which position one has to lie about (the imposition of new taxes), and which positions one must pander to in order to have a political career (the sacred nature of the flag). Particularly when combined with demographic data (which will be far easier in a two-way interactive system where even larger databases and more efficient access programs will be available), these opinion polls also inform political operatives of the most effective advertising levers to pull to get voters to support their candidate or smear their opponent. At best, a two-way system will produce politicians who are adept at pandering to impulsive public opinion. At worst, it will provide further data for the efficient manipulation of the people.

The social science of coordinating and manipulating people within organizations has also advanced significantly in recent years. Even as far back as 1951, Mills (one of the best futurists of the century) had the following take on the human relation's movement in management:

> The new (social) scientific management begins precisely where Taylor left off or was incomplete; students of "human relations in industry" have studied not lighting and clean toilets, but social cliques and good morale. For in so far as human factors are involved in efficient and untroubled production, the managerial demiurge must bring them under control. So, in factory and in office, the world to be managed increasingly includes the social setting, the human affairs, and the personality of man as worker. (Mills 1951, 233)

By becoming seemingly democratic, the system of authority is disguised and opposition to management (or government) becomes much more difficult to organize and sustain.

Bureaucracies are increasingly turning to the "human relations school" of management — with benefits, quality of work-life projects, beer busts, pep rallies, stock options, and worker participation — all to strengthen managerial authority. As noted in Chapter 4, the object of the human relations school is to give workers the illusion that they are in control and work in a caring environment in order to engender loyalty and commitment to the organization. Mills characterized the human relations school this way:

> The over-all formula of advice that the new ideology of 'human relations in business' contains runs to this effect: to make the worker happy, efficient, and co-operative, you must make the managers intelligent, rational, knowledgeable. It is the perspective of a managerial elite, disguised in the pseudo-objective language of engineers. It is advice to the personnel manager to relax his authoritative manner and widen his manipulative grip over the employees by understanding them better and countering their informal solidarities against management and exploiting these solidarities for smoother and less troublesome managerial efficiency. (Mills 1951, 235)

It is the movement of authority to manipulation, a system of control, that is more subtle, pervasive, effective, and efficient.

The new technologies and techniques much lauded by postindustrialists as liberating individuals from the hierarchies of old are technologies and techniques that enhance the efficiency and power of these same bureaucracies. Bureaucracies harness these technologies and techniques to efficiently attain their instrumental goals. Whether the goal is profit, collecting taxes, or intelligence, all else is subordinate to the bottom line.

New Infrastructure

Are modern industrial societies undergoing a qualitative change to a new mode of production? According to forecasters, postindustrialism is developing in our midst as industrialism is rapidly being transformed by technologies. However, their case is seriously weakened by their failure to offer any sort of coherent explanation as to what that new mode of production entails. The failure to agree even on a foundation (the term "postindustrial," after all, is simply a label that says what this new mode of production is not) is some indication that the term is almost devoid of any real substance.

Have these new technologies changed our social-technological relationships to the environment? We still take our energy and material needs from the environment through extractive activities. We still practice agriculture with industrial machinery and the liberal use of oil. We still do the bulk of our manufacturing within the factory system. Although postindustrialists can demonstrate that new manufacturing technologies have taken us beyond the assembly line, their equation of industrialism with labor-intensive, assembly-line manufacturing is flawed. Equating industrialism with assembly-line manufacturing is like equating physics with Newton. Industrialism is the use of science, technology, and rational social practices to manipulate the physical environment in order to produce goods. The use of microprocessors and robotics in the manufacture of goods is firmly in this tradition. The rise of the service economy, as we have seen, is rooted in the beginnings of industrialism. Nothing postulated by the postindustrialists represents a significant break with the past, with the industrial mode of production itself.

Anthropologists are right to caution us that we should not interpret massive social change, such as the agricultural revolution, as happening overnight. Despite the term "revolution" (which is used here to mean a qualitative change or a change in kind), the transition from hunting-and-gathering to horticulture occurred over many generations. Sociologists would do well to use similar caution in using the term "industrial revolution." Even though social change occurs more rapidly in the modern era, fundamental social change still takes place over generations.

With an imperfect understanding of history, postindustrialists posited an industrial society some 200 years old that was on the verge of transforming itself into a society based on something other than industrialism. In fact, although the industrial revolution is some 200 years old, industrial society is a relatively recent phenomenon. Kumar argued that the first real industrial society did not appear until about 1900, when slightly less than half of the population of Great Britain was involved in agriculture. I would go further than this. Great Britain in 1900 was still a society in transition, still largely organized around agrarian production. The first true industrial society — a society that was "fully" organized around industrialism as a mode of production — did not occur until 1945, when the United States emerged from World War II. (Again, this was a continuous process, one that we somewhat arbitrarily label and date as if it were a single event.) Since that time, American institutions, values, and ideologies have been undergoing rapid change to accommodate the needs of a rapidly intensifying industrial mode of production. Postindustrialists have interpreted this rapid change as the beginnings of a new type of society emerging from the old, when it can be more readily interpreted (and understood) as the intensification of industrialism itself.

Given the weaknesses of postindustrial "theory," some important questions to ask are, why has it gained so many adherents; why has it become an almost unquestioned assumption on the part of many business and political leaders; why is it a staple in our introductory sociology books, a cliché in almost every graduation speech of the last 20 years. There is no doubt that Western civilization is presently undergoing profound change within the industrial infrastructure. No doubt this change is affecting our social structure and culture. By viewing recent social changes as the intensification of industrialization, we have a wealth of social theory and historical experience to help us understand and guide these changes. Much of this theory and history urges us to be skeptical of progress — to consider the environmental, social, and human costs to the industrialization process, but viewing recent changes as the emergence of a new form of society has very different consequences. It gives us a new vision and a new ideology of technological and social progress.

As people in the West began to lose faith in the ideology of industrial progress, postindustrial theorists began to sell us on the idea of a glorious society based on a different mode of production. This new society would not have huge disparities in wealth. This new society would be much more democratic, less bureaucratic, much more productive, and provide a multitude of life-style choices and rewarding careers to its inhabitants. All we needed to do to achieve this future, many claimed, was to put our faith in new technologies and let social development take its course. The strongest adherents of postindustrialism come from backgrounds in business, engineering, and technology. Rather than a social theory, postindustrialism can be understood as an elaborate ideology developed to justify the status quo, capitalism, and the path we are presently on. It is a simple update of the idea of progress and a paean to technology. As such, it is a modern expression of the technological world view. It is by positing a new mode of production — a qualitative break with the past — that postindustrialists disconnect our future from our past. It is by ignoring human history (as they do ecology and social organization) that they can herald their brave new world.

9

Possibilities

This book is based on a theory. The first chapter presented and elaborated sociocultural materialism, a systems theory that incorporates insights from a variety of social theory traditions in an attempt to account for social origins, stability, and change. Theory is important. Through theory we can better grasp the basic organization of all societies to better understand our past as well as our present. Through theory we provide a structure that can help us organize seemingly isolated and random research findings, social facts, and explanations of cultural variations into a systemic view that provides clarity rather than confusion. The structure of theory enables us to approach complexity without oversimplification, to hypothesize causal relationships within a broad range of variables, and to guide us in our explorations of new issues. Theory provides a research agenda that can direct future empirical research, identify issues that need further clarification, which can refine, extend, or modify the theory as well as increase our understanding of the social world. It is only when there is a clear interaction between social theory and empirical research that theory can fulfill its promise. Society is a system, and good social theory attempts to interrelate the key elements of that system in a clear, forthright, and useful manner.

Sociocultural materialism is built on a foundation of materialism, on the mundane assumption that the way people go about making their living is a key element in understanding the social system. The claim is made that the interactions of a society with its natural environment (that is, material conditions) are an excellent starting point in understanding social stability and social change. The first and central task of any social system is to exploit its environment for the material resources that are needed to support life. The chief environmental constraints are the availability of energy and raw materials and the natural environment's tolerance for pollution.

The sociocultural practices by which society balances its needs with the environment are included in the infrastructure. Individuals who respond to the availability of needed resources (which are made known to them directly in traditional societies and indirectly through prices in industrial societies) make independent decisions (both conscious and unconscious) regarding family size and work habits. It is through the actions of individuals in response to the costs and benefits of productive and reproductive life that a society manipulates the amount of resources it requires. It is through these individual actions that the system adjusts by changing population size or intensifying the mode of production.

However, this is only a starting point. There is a complexity to sociocultural systems that resists a simple reduction of all phenomena to material conditions. The full exploration of social structure (human organizations and groups) and cultural superstructures (accumulated knowledge, ideologies, and beliefs) in interaction with each other and material conditions is needed to adequately reflect the complexities of sociocultural systems. It is the insistence on this point that has led me to modify Marvin Harris's theory of cultural materialism to better reflect structural and cultural factors in explaining sociocultural stability and change. In addition, by modifying the structural and superstructural components of Harris's perspective, it is better equipped to incorporate (or synthesize) a wide range of traditional sociological and anthropological perspectives into the body of the theory.

Fortunately, Max Weber's concepts and theories of bureaucracy and rationalization are an ideal fit with Harris's basic ecological theory. It was Weber's contention that bureaucracy was increasingly dominating the structures of modern Western societies. Weber also associated the rationalization process, or the increasing dominance of goal-oriented rational behavior in motivating individual action, with bureaucratization. Rationalization is a habit of thought that is fostered by bureaucratic organization. Weber considered bureaucracy as a specific example of rationalization applied to human organization. The intensification of the infrastructure can be considered a specific example of rationalization applied to our efforts to live within the constraints of the environment.

To summarize the general dynamics of the system: In order to wrest needed resources from a depleting environment, the mode of production intensifies. This intensification often produces more food, and thus population grows. The intensification of the infrastructure creates a need for the growth of formal organization to coordinate large numbers of people and complicated production processes. This growth of bureaucracy is at the expense of traditional groupings of kin and informal relationships. In accordance with Weber's theory, bureaucracy fosters the growth of goal-oriented rational behavior at the expense of behavior motivated by tradition, values, and emotions. This rationalization promotes the future growth of bureaucracy at the expense of traditional groups, both of which promote further intensification of the infrastructure. The engine of the system is one of environmental-infrastructural relationships. The reciprocal-causal interactions of the infrastructure with social structures and cultural superstructures provide the dynamics of sociocultural change.

Having detailed the structure and dynamics of the theory in the first chapter, Chapter 2, Sociocultural Evolution, examined the two signal events of social evolution — the agrarian and industrial revolutions — to both illustrate the explanatory power of the theory and to set the stage for an analysis of contemporary industrialism. The theory provided a comprehensive organization of the diversity of factors that social scientists have identified in their explanations of the social evolutionary process. The evidence gives primacy to such materialistic factors as resource availability, intensification beyond environmental sustainability, new technologies, and population pressures at the base of the evolutionary process. Structural and cultural factors in the form of increased commercial activities, reorganization of farm holdings, a storehouse of cultural knowledge and historical experience, a drive for greater efficiencies, and a willingness to abandon tradition were also identified as necessary systemic changes that interact with infrastructural intensification.

In Chapter 3, Structure of Authority, the argument is that the intensification of the infrastructure — that is, the growth of population and the complexity of production — have caused the growth in the size and power of structural bureaucracies and the weakening of traditional, primary groups. These bureaucracies are both public and private. Although their institutional goals are diverse, the methods by which their goals are achieved are not. A bureaucracy achieves its goals through the establishment of hierarchy, ever increasing division of labor, and rules based on impersonality (also called the rationalization process). By design, great authority is vested in those at the top of hierarchies, and the evidence is strong that this authority is becoming more concentrated, wider in scope, and more pervasive. The interests of elites clearly lie with a continued intensification of the production process. Intensification not only preserves but also enhances the power and position of elites. So pervasive is bureaucratic power and influence that economic growth in the pursuit of ever greater amounts of material wealth has become the unquestioned goal of the entire society.

It was also in Chapter 3 that Weber's irrationality factor was introduced. This is the tendency for bureaucracies to engage in actions that are irresponsible, often contrary to the long-term interests of both the social system and the very organization itself. There are several factors that cause bureaucracies to act in irrational ways:

a hierarchy of authority in which questions of orders and directions are discouraged;

a parceling out of specialized tasks and responsibilities;

a weakening of traditions, values, and social bonds that foster restraint;

a focus on being a part of the team; and

an overriding focus on efficiency in the attainment of the goals of an organization.

Rationally organized social arrangements bind individuals to the purpose of the organization. They are a means to coordinate the action of the many by submerging an individual's capacity to reason to the purpose of the organization. Thus, by design, they are instruments of control and manipulation (and if all else fails, tyranny) that seek to limit human action and freedom.

In Economic Rationalization (Chapter 4) the continuing rationalization of the American economy brought on by globalization was examined. Because of unique historical circumstances of World War II and its immediate aftermath, the American economy became far removed from the competition of ideal capitalism. Many American markets became dominated by huge corporations that were intent on maximizing profits without any real check on prices or any inducement to improve the quality of their goods and services from competitors. In effect, producers and consumers had a compact in which people received good jobs and wages in return for purchasing American goods and services that were high priced and often shoddy. Salaries and prices rose, the middle class grew, bureaucracies became more elaborate and layered, and corporations became larger and more centralized. Because of the lack of competition, technological innovations slowed, and there were no structural forces to promote lowered costs or improved quality.

With globalization came international competition, or a reintroduction of capitalism with a vengeance. Beginning in the early 1970s, American corporations have had to employ a number of rationalization strategies to stay competitive in domestic and international markets. These strategies have included downsizing, increasing use of automation, more reliance on contingency work, tightening coordination, and wage and benefit controls on the workers who remain. These rationalizing trends have been great for the bottom line, but they play havoc with the work and life of millions.

In Chapter 5, Erosion of Commitment, we examined some of the effects that continuing industrialization-rationalization has on the social and cultural life of citizens. The initial focus of the chapter was on the concept of the disintegrating impact of an increasing division of labor. It was Emile Durkheim's contention that an increasing division of labor (or specialization) led to a growth of individualism and a weakening of ties between people. With an increase in the division of labor, Durkheim predicted, society would disintegrate (or dis-integrate). Norms would lose much of their power and force; deviance and criminality would increase. Individuals would lose their sense of community and common purpose and identity with others. Consequently, rates of social participation would decline. Distrust and consequent delegitimation of authority would become widespread.

The division of labor, or extreme specialization, has increased dramatically in the United States since World War II. Most recently, as part of the continued rationalization of the social structure, millions of women have been pushed and pulled out of their traditional roles as mothers, homemakers, and caregivers for children. This has introduced the division of labor directly into millions of homes with the predictable results of rising divorce rates, an increasing number of single-parent households, and smaller family sizes. At the community level, the erosion of the social bond is seen in less participation in social organizations, a decline in commitment to community organizations, and a rise in the distrust of social institutions.

The themes of Chapter 6, Factual Regularities, and Chapter 7, Widening Gyre, are that multiple institutions within the American social structure are slipping the bonds of traditional, emotional, and value constraints in order to efficiently achieve organizational goals. Many institutions have long had rationalized components, but all were also characterized by ethical, traditional, or emotional constraints on rationalized activity. The constraints of tradition, emotions, and value orientations are increasingly ignored (or worse, not even thought of in the mind of individuals) in the drive for the efficient attainment of goals. Rationalized strategies are increasingly being used in the service, government, and nonprofit sectors of the economy, as these organizations face tighter budgets and a rising ideological tide of recommitment to the principles of efficiency. Specifically, we examined the rationalization of health care, agriculture, higher education, and political campaigns in American society. However, examples of the rationalization of traditional elements of our structure are numerous — warfare; journalism; professional, amateur, and college sports; and entertainment to name a few. As with the economic sectors of the social structure, an exclusive focus on short-term goals — whether they are for profit, productivity, or simply winning at all costs — are often destroyers of the very social system that sustains these institutions. Without traditional constraints on our behavior we rely almost exclusively on external constraints to our actions. The erosion of the social bond imperils both freedom and social order.

Chapter 8, New Ideology, argued that, contrary to the assertions of many futurists, the foundation of the modern sociocultural system is still one of industrialism. Although there is no doubt that we are in the midst of profound changes in our social structures and culture, these changes are an extension of industrialism — they do not represent a qualitatively different type of society. The changes wrought by industrial intensification cannot possibly lead us to a more democratic, egalitarian, or just society. Such a society, if it is to be achieved, can only be attained by the deliberate actions of human beings working toward it. Postindustrialism, I claim, represents the new ideology of progress, an ideology that serves to justify and promote the continued intensification-rationalization process.

In this, the final chapter, I want to briefly summarize the characteristics of the American sociocultural system and examine some possibilities for our future. The bonds of tradition, emotional commitment, and values appear to have loosened. Rational action in the pursuit of institutional and personal goals (however they are defined) appear to be increasingly unchecked from within. Are there possible system or human limitations on further rationalization — on a further loosening of traditional social constraints on human action? Can the rationalization process be reversed?

INDUSTRIAL INTENSIFICATION

Industrial growth can be expected to continue for the foreseeable future. The dominant institutions in our society, both government and business, are firmly committed to economic growth. Fundamental reforms that challenge the existence of the elite simply cannot be granted. The present system is based on continued economic growth; such growth is essential to the continuation of the system. Stopping growth, or an equilibrium state, is not an option without prior social collapse, revolution, or both.

In response to a deteriorating environment and a declining standard of living, as well as the need for growth, industrial technology will become increasingly sophisticated, scientific, and efficient. What is workable (in technical and economic feasibility) in nuclear fusion, synthetic fuels, superconductors, solar energy, ocean mining, and the substitution of materials for those depleted will be developed and deployed. Pollution and depletion increasingly will be managed on a global scale. As the crisis continues to intensify, governments and international organizations will act to limit pollution and environmental depletion. However, the ecological principles employed in fashioning the industrial infrastructure will be the principles that are compatible with industrial growth and the other interests of existing economic and governmental elites.

By committing ourselves to economic growth, we are betting that technological development can be achieved that will tap into almost infinite supplies of energy and raw materials, with no delays in its development and deployment, at affordable prices, and with minimal physical costs to the environment. In order to offset the costs of depletion and pollution, our technology will have to become more complex and sophisticated. For example,

Technology will be called upon to tap into new energy sources, to go farther and deeper in our search for raw materials, and to restore parts of our environment that have already been destroyed.

Technology will have to provide food, clothing, shelter, and the industrial "good life" for more than 70 percent of the world population that currently lives in Third World nations.

New technologies have the additional burden of providing ever-increasing amounts of energy and raw materials to fuel an expansion of existing industrial states. This expansion is necessary to provide food, energy, and shelter to an expanding population as well as increased material wealth to our descendants.

New technology will have to provide ever more efficient pollution and control methods to compensate for the growth.

Personally, I place great faith in science and technology. I am aware of the potential benefits of the computer revolution and the pending biological revolution, as well as potential advances in agricultural science, new energy sources, and new sources of raw materials. Still, there are limits. Technological development may be able to forestall the "overshoot and collapse" mode for the foreseeable future, but it, too, is subject to physical limits.

Although substitutes, recycling, and conservation measures will buy time for industrial society, they cannot provide the raw materials needed for continued growth. Although technological developments may be able to tap lower grades of ore and new energy sources, they are by no means assured; they are likely to require huge inputs of energy and capital to develop and deploy; they are still bound by the ultimate limits of the earth. Furthermore, new technologies have to be technically and economically feasible. Technologies such as improved crop strains, more efficient use of nonrenewable resources, improved land management, and pollution control are capable of extending the physical limits to growth, but we cannot expect them to overcome environmental limits permanently. (Technology, too, is subject to physical laws.) No one really knows how far (or how long) technology can stretch environmental limits (or even what the limits are). Further intensification is based on the bet that we can do it indefinitely. It is quite a bet—we are gambling with our future.

It is possible that we will come up against real environmental limits to industrial intensification in the next century. Other societies have reached the physical limits of their mode of production and have collapsed as a result (Flannery 1994). We are as dependent upon environmental resources as any society in the past. Aside from collapse, the real possibility exists that despite an expanding industrial economy and ever more sophisticated technology, living standards for the greater part of humanity will decline (some argue that this has already begun). This by itself could cause a massive disruption in sociocultural systems.

However, putting aside the unknowable issues of environmental limits and the potential of technology to stretch them, it is evident that industrialism will continue to intensify for the foreseeable future. Given the history of industrialization and its effects on the rest of the sociocultural system, this is likely to lead to the growth in the power of bureaucracy and further disruption of traditional institutions and values.

PRIMARY GROUPS

As industrialization continues to intensify, primary groups such as the family and community will continue to lose many of their functions, which has the potential to radically alter social life. Perhaps the greatest change in modern society in the last 30 years has been the shift in employment of married women from domestic and child-care services within the home to employment in the market economy. In large part, this shift in employment has been caused by an attempt to maintain middle-class living standards in the modern economy (Harris 1981, 76–97). (Indeed, it seems that the employment of greater numbers of women is the primary way American families have maintained family income in the last 20 years, as personal incomes have remained remarkably stagnant.) Another factor in the employment of women outside the home has been the growth of bureaucratic and service jobs caused by industrial intensification (Harris 1981, 76–97). At first, industrial intensification weakened the extended family system. Emphasis on the nuclear family unit was essential for social and geographic mobility. Now, with both husband and wife working outside the home, this mobility is increasingly important for each. Further industrial intensification puts the nuclear family itself at risk.

One impact of industrialization on the family is smaller families. Because the state forbids child labor outside the home and increasingly provides economic security in old age, and in an advanced industrial society in which married women are employed outside the home and the cost of raising a child is a major financial commitment (and consumerism is a major value), there are even fewer reasons to have children. Having no or few children makes the marriage bond less stable. Beyond marriage, smaller family sizes will have implications for the extended family as well. Even without factoring in geographic and social mobility, after several generations of one or two children, there will be fewer people in one's extended family with whom to interact. Again, it is possible that there are some limits, in this case human limits, to the further weakening of primary groups.

SECONDARY ORGANIZATION

Socialization increasingly will take place within secondary organizations. As married women continue to work outside the home, daycare, preschool, and after-school programs will continue to proliferate. Socialization in secondary organizations at such an early age (many daycare facilities now routinely care for infants as young as two weeks) teaches the child to live within bureaucratic structures. This increasing rationalization of socialization will speed social change, as well as expose our youth at an earlier age to the direct influence of elites. In the past, family and community influences on childhood socialization acted as a brake on rapid social change. For example, intellectuals, churches, and schools could preach tolerance and acceptance of different races, but the family that preached racism had a more direct and lasting influence on the formation of a child's personality. With the advent of daycare, the balance began to change. These secondary organizations, which are organized along rational lines and subject to government regulation and inspection, socialize children in accordance with the latest mores and conventions. Mass media programming aimed at children and children's books and movies promote the same message. Although a child may be exposed to conflicting messages from family and peers, the influence of these more traditional agents of socialization is waning.

The United States and other industrial nations are rapidly undergoing a transformation in employment from the production of goods to the production of services and information. There are several reasons for this trend. The function of technology is in its application to traditional agriculture and manufacturing to make them more efficient and productive. The impact of the application of high technology in these areas has been (and will continue to be) to reduce the number of workers needed. Domestic capital is flowing overseas at an increasing rate in search of cheap labor and more lax environmental and occupational safety laws. Production jobs that remain in advanced industrial societies are becoming automated as industrial companies attempt to reduce their wage expenses in order to maintain or increase existing profit levels.

As industrialization continues to intensify, demands for geographic and social mobility will continue to weaken the extended family as well as the basic nuclear family, thus putting even more demand on the service industries. Government and the market economy are providing services that used to be performed by families or communities. Most of these service jobs are relatively low-pay, low-skill occupations, such as kitchen helpers, custodians, and nurses' aides and orderlies.

The bulk of the much-vaunted information occupations are the white-collar bureaucratic jobs of old. As industrial technologies become more complex and require ever greater inputs of capital to purchase and operate, corporations become larger and the need for bureaucracy to coordinate and control far-flung empires becomes more acute. As international competition becomes more intense, we can expect corporate bureaucracy to become more efficient by employing more computer and communications technology to meet the challenge.

The application of high technology to service and information occupations is lowering the overall skill levels of the workforce, making people poorer and less educated. The new wave of automation and computerization currently sweeping through traditional bureaucracies and service organizations is done in the name of efficiency. Electronic workstations and the like are not only more efficient in performing work tasks, they are also ideal for monitoring employee performance. They offer the hope to the corporate manager of controlling the most unpredictable part of the work process — human performance. A large part of the rationalization and bureaucratization detailed earlier is also the direct consequence of a slowing of economic growth itself. Governments, educational institutions, and other service organizations can no longer count on an ever-expanding tax base — bureaucratic rationalization can be seen as an attempt to maximize efficiency with limited resources.

Recent structural changes made in response to the intensifying infrastructure also point toward increasing control through bureaucratization and the resulting oligarchy. Government and corporate growth in the twentieth century has been phenomenal. Whatever the outcome of the environmental crisis, whether the process results in environmental collapse of technological innovations that "overcome" environmental constraints, governments and corporations will increase their power to deal with the crisis. Bureaucratic control is based on manipulation rather than terror. Modern technology and techniques have led to a concentration of economic and political power in huge bureaucracies that increasingly control social life. This control is hidden, manipulative, and almost inconspicuous, and thus it is extremely efficient and effective. In the name of welfare, efficiency, the environment, taxation, and education, to name but a few of the laudable goals, administration has expanded and will continue to expand in power and influence. The prospects for democracy in such a society are dismal.

It is probable that there are structural limits to the amount of centralization of control that can efficiently take place in a complex industrial society. The former Soviet Union and other highly centralized economies probably exceeded this limit. Industrial capitalism is relatively decentralized when compared to the Soviet model. For coordination capitalism relies much more on markets, somewhat autonomous local bureaucracies (in terms of day to day operations), an almost exclusive focus on efficiency throughout the organizational structure, and advanced technologies of coordination, manipulation, and communication. Because of this reliance it is likely that industrial democracy will remain within any structural limits on efficient centralization.

SUPERSTRUCTURE

A major theme of this book has been on the rise of rationalization or what could be called the increasing dominance of a technological world view. The argument has been made that industrial intensification leads to the bureaucratization of structure, which promotes the rationalization process. Furthermore, and just as important, rationalization promotes further bureaucratization, both of which encourage further intensification. People's perceptions of the world and their place in it are greatly affected by how they go about making their living. By adopting an industrial mode of production we begin to view the world — as well as other people — as raw material, to be manipulated and exploited for our own ends. Goal oriented rationality becomes our habitual way of thought. To state this in more colloquial terms (or perhaps, more poetically): "Once, the governing human metaphor was pastoral or agricultural, and it clarified, and so preserved in human care, the natural cycles of birth, growth, death, and decay. But modern humanity's governing metaphor is that of the machine. Having placed ourselves in charge of Creation, we began to mechanize both the Creation itself and our conception of it. We began to see the whole Creation merely as raw material, to be transformed by machines into a manufactured Paradise" (Berry 1977, 56). Weber called this process rationalization; Wendell Berry called it a change of "governing metaphor"; Jacques Ellul labeled it the rise of "technique." It has become the dominant way that industrial people perceive their world.

According to C. Wright Mills, among the most important questions to ask of any society are, "What varieties of men and women now prevail in this society and in this period? And what varieties are coming to prevail? In what ways are they selected and formed, liberated and repressed, made sensitive and blunted?" (Mills 1959, 7). Asking these questions with respect to the future of industrial society is not reassuring. Our lives are being spent increasingly in rational, secondary organizations designed to perform like machines; the goals and values of economic elites dominate these hierarchical organizations. As we have seen, in response to declines in living standards, we have intensified industrial activity and put greater stress on bureaucratic efficiency in our dominant institutions. The efficient operation of these organizations depends on workers' ability to perform the narrowly specialized role they have been assigned to maximize organizational efficiency. Clients of the organization (or patients, or customers, or students) are likewise dehumanized and treated as categories based on status rather than as human beings. Participation in these organizations demands a rational mind-set, a habit of thought that has become our way of perceiving the physical and social world. A society dominated by such organizations, one that socializes its children into these organizations at an earlier age is going to inculcate and reinforce men and women whose values can be stated on a balance sheet.

Many find the existing sociocultural system unsatisfying. It is arguable that more people are either dropping out of participation in the system or searching for alternative lifestyles. Millions of others seem to be going through the motions (playing the game) without commitment or purpose. Some detect rising levels of disaffection among our youth. The underclass, too, appears to be increasing in numbers, and the middle class is in decline. Perhaps the rise of alienation, cynicism, and apathy indicate that more people are no longer finding either physical or psychological gratification in the existing industrial order. If so, it may be the social actions of the disaffected (shades of Marx's proletariat) that will bring change to the sociocultural system.

At the same time, it would be a mistake to suppose that a technological world view completely dominates industrial societies, even among those who fully participate in the system. There are still traditional and religious institutions. There are many who are still guided by traditional and religious values that still have a significant effect on the rest of the sociocultural system. There are deeply religious men and women in our society who are horrified with recent sociocultural change and strive to interpret their vision of a just society into social action. Much of this social activism is particularly effective at the local level — food banks, shelters for the homeless, free clinics. There are other advocates of social justice who are guided by more secular values, and again, these men and women have some success. Tradition and religion may be waning; their current role in the world could be interpreted as rear guard activities — pale remnants of what once was, but perhaps there will be a religious rebirth or a revival of the humanist tradition as human limits of rationalization are reached.

Recent history has seen the rapid rise of a new alternative world view — that of ecology. The ecology movement, as it has evolved in the last 30 years, has become ever more consciously opposed to the dominant, technological world view. What began as an environmental critique of certain industrial abuses quickly broadened to a general hostility toward the industrial system's exploitation and degradation of the earth, and further still to a general critique of industrial society itself. The appeal of the ecology movement is based on a growing skepticism of both technology and the ability of present-day institutions to control its use. It is connected with a general feeling of unease about the future of industrial society. It is not, at least in its broader social expression, based solely on ecological science. The movement contains elements of romanticism, religious values, ethics, revolutionary politics, and belief in the imminence of the Second Coming, to name a few. What holds the movement together is a common world view, a holistic world view that is based on the interconnections between systems.

The ecology movement increasingly is a force to be reckoned with by both government and industry. Elements of the movement have been institutionalized. Its ideology has demonstrated its power to mobilize people to at least consider values other than immediate material benefit; at times it has even inspired some to act in an altruistic manner. As industrialization continues to intensify, the movement can be expected to broaden and strengthen. It is perhaps in the resolution of this struggle between two competing world views that the future of industrial society will be decided.

We are both creatures and creators of sociocultural systems. Even in a sociocultural system that increasingly institutionalizes and rewards goal-oriented rational behavior in pursuit of wealth and material symbols of status, there are other possibilities. It is fitting to close with a quote from Weber, who also engaged in speculation on the future possibilities of industrial systems. Although Weber had a foreboding of an iron cage of bureaucracy and rationality, he recognized that human beings are not mere subjects molded by sociocultural forces.

> No one knows who will live in this cage in the future, or whether at the end of this tremendous development entirely new prophets will arise, or there will be a great rebirth of old ideas and ideals or, if neither, mechanized petrifaction embellished with a sort of convulsive self-importance. For of the last stage of this

cultural development, it might well be truly said: "Specialists without spirit, sensualists without heart; this nullity imagines that it has obtained a level of civilization never before achieved." (Weber 1921, 181)

There are still many possibilities, many possible futures. Ours could be one that we choose.

References

Abate, Tom. 1998. Why huge corporate marriages are busting out all over; firms think size matters, says one merger tracker. *San Francisco Chronicle*, July 30, p. D1.

Barkume, Megan. 1998. College and university faculty. In *The Occupational Outlook Handbook.* U.S. Department of Labor, retrieved October 12, 1998, http://stats.bls.gov/oco/ocos066.htm#outlook.

Bernstein, Aaron. 1996. Is America becoming more of a class society? *Business Week*, 3464 (February 26): 86–91.

Berry, Wendell. 1977. *The Unsettling of America.* San Francisco: Sierra Club.

Birenbaum, Arnold. 1993. Managed care: what's in store for U.S.? *USA TODAY: The Magazine for the American Scene*, 122, (November): 20–22.

Birnbaum, Jeffrey. 1997. The power 25. *Fortune*, 136 (December 8): 144–152.

Boustead, Thomas. 1997. The U.S. economy to 2006. *Monthly Labor Review*, 120 (November): 6–23.

Brady, John Joseph. 1996. *Bad Boy: The Life and Politics of Lee Atwater.* New York: Addison-Wesley.

Breslow, Marc, Abby Sher, & Leslie Brokaw. 1996. Government of, by, and for the wealthy. *Dollars & Sense*, 206 (July–August): 23–28.

Brown, Lester R., Hal Kane, & David M. Roodman. 1995. *Vital Signs: The Trends That Are Shaping Our Future, 1994.* New York: W. W. Norton.

Burnham, David. 1980. *The Rise of the Computer State.* New York: Vintage.

Carneiro, Robert L. (ed.). 1967. Editor's introduction. In *The Evolution of Society: Selections from Herbert Spencer's Principles of Sociology.* Chicago: University of Chicago Press.

Carville, James, Mary Matalin, & Peter Knobler. 1994. *All's Fair: Love, War, and Running for President*. New York: Touchstone Books.

Chronicle of Higher Education. 1998 Almanac Issue, 45 (August 28).

Clift, Eleanor & Tom Brazaitis. 1996. *War Without Bloodshed: The Art of Politics*. New York: Scribner.

Cohen, Mark. 1977. *The Food Crisis in Prehistory: Over Population and the Origins of Agriculture*. New Haven, CT: Yale University Press.

Demo, D., & A. C. Acock. 1993. Family diversity and the division of domestic labor: How much have things really changed? *Family Relations*, 42, pp. 326–327.

de Tocqueville, Alexis. 1835. *Democracy in America*. Robert D. Meffner (ed.). New York: New American Library.

The doctor is in — online: Hospital company experiments with telemedicine. 1997. *Orlando Sentinel*, May 3, pp. C–1, C–9.

Domhoff, G. William. 1967. *Who Rules America?* Englewood Cliffs, NJ: Prentice Hall.

Drew, Elizabeth. 1997. *Whatever It Takes: The Real Struggle for Political Power in America*. New York: Viking Press.

Durkheim, Emile. 1893. *The Division of Labor in Society*. Translated by George Simpson. New York: The Free Press.

Durkheim, Emile. 1897. *Suicide: A Study in Sociology*. Translated by John A. Spaulding & George Simpson. New York: The Free Press.

Dye, Thomas R. 1983. *Who's Running America? The Reagan Years*. Englewood Cliffs, NJ: Prentice Hall.

Dye, Thomas R. 1986. *Who's Running America? The Conservative Years*. Englewood Cliffs, NJ: Prentice Hall.

The Economist. 1997a. 344 (September 20): S7–S10.

The Economist. 1997b. 342 (January 18): 23–26.

Eisenstodt, Gale. 1993. Information power. *Forbes*, 151 (June 21): 44–45.

Ellul, Jacques 1964. *The Technological Society*. Translated by John Wilkinson. New York: Alfred A. Knopf.

Etzioni, Amitai. 1984. *Capital Corruption: The New Attack on American Democracy*. New York: Harcourt, Brace, Jovanovich.

Flannery, Tim F. 1994. *The Future Eaters*. Port Melbourne, Australia: Reed.

Freund, Julien. 1969. *The Sociology of Max Weber*. New York: Vintage.

Gates, William. 1997. *The Road Ahead*. New York: Penguin Books.

Gigy, L. & J. B. Kelly. 1992. Reasons for divorce: perspectives of divorcing men and women. *Journal of Divorce and Remarriage*, 18, pp. 174–175.

Gittleman, Maury & Mary Joyce. 1995. Earnings mobility in the United States, 1967–91. *Monthly Labor Review*, 118 (September): 3–13.

Glenn, Norval. 1997. *Closed Hearts, Closed Minds: The Textbook Story of Marriage*. New York: Institute for American Values.

Goldschmidt, Walter. 1990. *The Human Career: The Self in the Symbolic World.* Cambridge: Basil Blackwell.

Gutmann, Myron P. 1988. *Toward the Modern Economy: Early Industry in Europe 1500–1800.* Philadelphia, PA: Temple University Press.

Halberstam, David. 1986. *The Reckoning.* New York: Avon Books.

Harrington, Michael. 1976. *The Twilight of Capitalism.* New York: Touchstone.

Harlow, Harry F. 1959. Love in infant monkeys. *Scientific American,* June, pp. 2–8.

Harris, Marvin. 1978. *Cows, Pigs, Wars, and Witches: The Riddles of Culture.* New York: Vintage.

Harris, Marvin. 1977. *Cannibals and Kings: The Origins of Cultures.* New York: Vintage.

Harris, Marvin. 1979. *Cultural Materialism: The Struggle for a Science of Culture.* New York: Random House.

Harris, Marvin. 1981. *America Now: The Anthropology of a Changing Culture.* New York: Simon and Schuster.

Harris, Marvin. 1995. Anthropology and postmodernism. In *Science, Materialism, and the Study of Culture,* Martin F. Murphy, and Maxine Margolis (eds.). Gainesville: University Press of Florida.

Harwood, Richard. 1996. Why are Americans apathetic to political money scandals? *The Paducah Sun,* September 8, p. 4.

Heilbroner, Robert. 1980. *An Inquiry Into the Human Prospect, Updated and Reconsidered for the 1980s.* New York: W. W. Norton.

Hendren, John. 1997. Employees say Columbia/HCA went overboard after profits. *The Paducah Sun,* September 9, p. 3A.

Hendren, John. 1998. Horror stories drive debate over HMOs. *The Paducah Sun,* August 21, p. 7B.

Howard, Robert. 1985. *Brave New Workplace.* New York: Viking.

Hudson, Pat. 1992. *The Industrial Revolution.* London: Edward Arnold.

Hudson, Terese. 1996. The lobbyists. *Hospital & Health Networks,* 70 (October 5): 46–50.

Hutchings, Vicky. 1989. On the funny farm. *New Statesman & Society,* 2 (January 20): 13–14.

Ilg, Randy E. 1995. The changing face of farm employment. *Monthly Labor Review,* 118 (April): 3–12.

Is the American worker getting shafted? 1996. *U.S. News & World Report,* 120 (January 22): 44–46.

Jenkins Kent, Jr. 1977. Learning to love those expensive campaigns: who profits? TV stations and consultants. *U.S. News & World Report,* 122 (March 10): 26–28.

Kalish, David E. 1998. Coming pain of technology highlighted by Bell strike. *The Paducah Sun,* August 11, p. 8A.

Kumar, Krishan. 1978. *Prophecy and Progress.* New York: Penguin.

Landis, David S. 1969. *The Unbound Prometheus: Technological Change and Industrial Development in Western Europe from 1750 to the Present.* London: Cambridge University Press.

Lasch, Christopher. 1979. *The Culture of Narcissism.* New York: Warner.

Lenski, Gerhard. 1966. *Power and Privilege: A Theory of Social Statification.* New York: McGraw-Hill.

Lenski, Gerhard, Patrick Nolan, & Jean Lenski. 1995. *Human Societies: An Introduction to Macrosociology.* New York: McGraw-Hill.

Leo, John. 1997. The answer is 45 cents. *U.S. News & World Report,* 122 (April 21): 14.

Levine, Art. 1997. The "conniving worm" factor. *U.S. News & World Report,* 122 (March 10): 29–30.

Light, Donald W. 1994. Managed care: False and real solutions. *Lancet,* 344 (October 29): 1197–1199.

Lugaila, Terry. 1992. Households, families, and children: A 30-year perspective. *Current Population Reports,* 28 (November): 23–181.

Magaziner, Ira C. & Robert Reich. 1983. *Minding America's Business.* New York: Vintage.

Mahar, Maggie. 1994. Tomorrow's hospital. *Barron's,* 12 (January).

Malthus, T. Robert. 1798. *The Principle of Population.* Frank Elwell (ed.), retrieved October 12, 1998, http://msumusik.mursuky.edu/~felwell/http/malthus/Index.htm.

Manno, Bruno V. 1995. Remedial education: Replacing the double standard with real standards. *Change,* 27, pp. 47–49.

Marx, Karl. 1859. *A Contribution to the Critique of Political Economy,* retrieved October 20, 1998. http://csf.colorado.edu/psn/marx/.

Marx, Karl. 1963. *Karl Marx: Early Writings.* Translated and edited by T. B. Bottomore. New York: McGraw-Hill.

Marx, Karl. 1972. *The Essential Writings.* Frederic L. Bender, (ed.). Boulder, CO: Westview.

Marx, Karl and Friedrich Engels. 1845. *The German Ideology.* C. J. Arthur (ed.). New York: International Publishers.

McCarthy, Michael. 1994. HMO loses US $89.3 million lawsuit. *Lancet,* 343 (January): 106–107.

McCormick, Brian. 1994. Court upholds HMO's right to deny liver transplant. *American Medical News,* 37 (September): 4.

McKibben, Bill. 1998. A special moment in history. *Atlantic Monthly,* May, pp. 55–78.

McNeill, William H. 1993. *A History of the Human Community.* Englewood Cliffs, NJ: Prentice Hall.

Menosky, Joseph A. 1984. Computer worship. *Science,* 84 (May): 40–46.

Merline, John W. 1994. Making money by denying health care. *Consumers' Research Magazine*, 77 (September): 10–15.

Meyer, Harris. 1994. Insurance giants bet on managed care. *American Medical News*, 37 (February): 3.

Michels, Robert. 1915. *Political Parties: A Sociological Study of the Oligarchical Tendencies of Modern Democracy*. Translated by Eden Paul and Cedar Paul. New York: The Free Press.

Milgram, Stanley. 1974. *Obedience to Authority: An Experimental View*. New York: Harper & Row.

Miller, Ken. 1997. How the merger boom will end: History's biggest takeover wave is reshaping the U.S. economy. *Fortune*, 136 (October 27): 279–281.

Mills, C. Wright. 1951. *White Collar: The American Middle Classes*. New York: Oxford University Press.

Mills, C. Wright. 1956. *The Power Elite*. New York: Oxford University Press.

Mills, C. Wright. 1958. *The Causes of World War Three*. London: Secker & Warburg.

Mills, C. Wright. 1959. *The Sociological Imagination*. New York: Oxford University Press.

Mitka, Mike. 1994a. Boom year. *American Medical News*, 37 (January): 2, 29.

Mitka, Mike. 1994b. Managed care plays big role in group practice. *American Medical News*, 37 (November): 10.

Mitka, Mike. 1994c. HMO enrollment tops 50 million. *American Medical News*, 37 (December): 3.

Mittelhauser, Mark. 1998. The outlook for college graduates, 1996–2006: Prepare yourself. *Occupational Outlook Quarterly*, 42 (Summer): 3.

Morris, Dick. 1997. *Behind the Oval Office: Winning the Presidency in the Nineties*. New York: Random House.

Nader, Ralph. 1965. *Unsafe at Any Speed: The Designed-in Dangers of the American Automobile*. New York: Grossman.

Naisbitt, John. 1982. *Megatrends*. New York: Warner.

National Center for Health Statistics. 1995. Annual summary of births, marriages, divorces, and death. Monthly *Vital Statistics Report*. Hyattsville, MD: U.S. Public Health Sevice.

Orwell, George. 1946. *Animal Farm: A Fairy Story*. New York: New American Library.

Parenti, Michael. 1978. *Power and the Powerless*. New York: St. Martin's Press.

Pressler, Margaret Webb. 1997. Wal-Mart plays well on wall street. *The Paducah Sun*, December 1, p. 6B.

Putnam, Robert D. 1995. Bowling alone: America's declining social capital. *Current*, 373 (June): 3–9.

Reich, Robert B. 1991. *The Work of Nations: Preparing Ourselves for 21st Century Capitalism*. New York: Alfred A. Knopf.

Rauch, Johnathan. 1995. *Demosclerosis; The Silent Killer of American Government*. New York: Times Books.

Riesman, David. 1980. *On Higher Education.* San Francisco: Josey-Bass.

Rifkin, Jeremy. 1995. *The End of Work: The Decline of the Global Labor Force and the Dawn of the Post-Market Era.* New York: G. P. Putnam's Sons.

Rice crackers. 1993. *The Economist,* 328 (August 7): 58.

Ritzer, George. 1995. *Expressing America: A Critique of the Global Credit Card Society.* Thousand Oaks, CA: Pine Forge Press.

Rollins, Ed & Tom Defrank. 1996. *Bare Knuckles and Back Rooms: My Life in American Politics.* New York: Broadway Books.

Rose, Stephen J. 1996. The truth about social mobility. *Challenge,* 39, (May): 4–8.

Rust, Michael. 1997. Manipulating the candidate. *Insight on the News,* 13 (March 10): 8–12.

Salant, Jonathan D. 1998. Lobbyists spent $1.17 billion in '97, study says. *The Paducah Sun,* July 8, p. 3A.

Saluter, Arlene. 1991. *Marital status and living arrangements: March 1990.* U.S. Bureau of the Census, Current Population Reports, Series P-20, No. 450. Washington, DC: U.S. Government Printing Office.

Shirer, William L. 1960. *The Rise and Fall of the Third Reich: A History of Nazi Germany,* vol. 2. New York: Simon and Schuster.

Spencer, Herbert. 1885. *The Evolution of Society, Selections from Herbert Spencer's Principles of Sociology.* Robert L. Carneiro (ed.). Chicago, IL: University of Chicago Press.

Spitz, Rene A. 1965. *The First Year of Life: A Psychoanalytic Study of Normal and Deviant Development of Object Relations.* New York: International Universities Press.

Stark, Rodney. 1994. *Sociology.* Belmont, CA: Wadsworth.

Stengel, Richard & Eric Pooley. 1996. Masters of the message: Inside the high-tech machine that set Clinton and Dole polls apart. *Time,* November 18, pp. 76–92.

Taylor, Dennis. 1996. Upcoming Adia, Ecco merger to create a personnel giant. *The Business Journal,* 14 (December 2): 4.

Toeffler, Alvin. 1981. *The Third Wave.* New York: Bantam.

U.S. Bureau of the Census. 1993. *Statistical Abstract of the United States, 1993* (113 ed.). Washington, DC: U.S. Government Printing Office.

U.S. Bureau of the Census. 1995. *Statistical Abstract of the United States, 1995* (115 ed.). Washington, DC: U.S. Government Printing Office.

U.S. Bureau of the Census. 1998. *Statistical Abstract of the United States, 1998* (118 ed.). Washington, DC: U.S. Government Printing Office.

U.S. Department of Energy web site. Human radiation experiments. http://tis-nt.eh.doe.gov/ohre/index.html, accessed July 30, 1998.

Vander Veer, Joseph B., Jr. 1997. How my practice profile almost got me fired. *Medical Economics,* 74 (August 11): 111–115.

Weber, Max. 1921. *Max Weber on Law in Economy and Society.* Max Rheinstein (ed.). Translated by Edward Shils and Max Rheinstein. New York: Simon and Schuster.

Weber, Max. 1904. *The Protestant Ethic and the Spirit of Capitalism.* Translated by Talcott Parsons. New York: Charles Scribner's Sons.

Weber, Max. 1946. *From Max Weber.* Translated and edited by H. H. Gerth and C. Wright Mills. New York: Galaxy.

Welles, Edward O. 1993. When Wal-Mart comes to town. *Inc.*, 15 (July): 76–78.

Wholey, Douglas R., Jon B. Christianson, & Susan M. Sanchez. 1993. The effect of physician and corporate interests on the formation of health maintenance organizations. *American Journal of Sociology*, 99 (July): 164–200.

Winner, Langdon. 1984. Mythinformation, http://www.eco-action.org/ot/mythin.htmy, retrieved August 3, 1999.

Woolhandler, Steffie & David U. Himmelstein. 1994. Giant H.M.O. "A" or giant H.M.O. "B." *Nation*, 259 (September 19): 265–268.

Wright, J. Patrick. 1979. *On A Clear Day You Can See General Motors: John Z. De Lorean's Look Inside the Automotive Giant.* New York: Avon Books.

Wright, Richard A. 1996. *A Brief History of the First 100 Years of the Automobile Industry in the United States.* The Auto Channel: http: //www. theautochannel.com/content/mania/industry/history/chap1.html

Wright, Robert. 1995. Hyper democracy: Washington isn't dangerously disconnected from the people; the trouble may be it's too plugged in. *Time*, 145 (January 23): 14–22.

Index

ABOUT THE AUTHOR

Frank W. Elwell is Professor of Sociology and Chairman of the Department of Anthropology, Sociology, and Social Work at Murray State University. He teaches social problems, social theory, and cultural ecology and is the author of *The Evolution of the Future* (Praeger, 1991).